THE
PROPHETIC
RESPONSIBILITY

THE
PROPHETIC
RESPONSIBILITY

MATTHEW L. STEVENSON III

CHARISMA
HOUSE

Most Charisma House Book Group products are available at special quantity discounts for bulk purchase for sales promotions, premiums, fund-raising, and educational needs. For details, write Charisma House Book Group, 600 Rinehart Road, Lake Mary, Florida 32746, or telephone (407) 333-0600.

The Prophetic Responsibility by Matthew L. Stevenson III
Published by Charisma House
Charisma Media/Charisma House Book Group
600 Rinehart Road
Lake Mary, Florida 32746
www.charismahouse.com

Visit the author's websites at matthewstevensonworldwide.com and matthewstevensonbooks.com.

Library of Congress Cataloging-in-Publication Data

Names: Stevenson, Matthew L., author.
Title: The prophetic responsibility / by Matthew L. Stevenson III, EdD
Description: Lake Mary : Charisma House, 2019. | Includes bibliographical
   references.
Identifiers: LCCN 2019023866 (print) | LCCN 2019023867 (ebook) | ISBN
   9781629995311 (trade paperback) | ISBN 9781629995328 (ebook)
Subjects: LCSH: Prophecy--Christianity. | Prophets.
Classification: LCC BR115.P8 S74 2019 (print) | LCC BR115.P8 (ebook) |
   DDC 231.7/45--dc23
LC record available at https://lccn.loc.gov/2019023866
LC ebook record available at https://lccn.loc.gov/2019023867

19 20 21 22 23 — 987654321
Printed in the United States of America

To my children, Micah, Naila, and Karis,
and to my amazing wife, Kamilah

Contents

Where Have All the Prophets Gone?

ANYONE WHO KNOWS me knows I have a strong conviction concerning the prophetic. I have always said that no matter where life takes me, I will always know there is a God because of what I have experienced, what I have seen, and what I have encountered by the power of the prophetic word.

Additionally, God's prophets have been a vital part of everything God has ever done on planet earth. Amos 3:7 says, "Surely the Lord GOD will do nothing, but he revealeth his secret unto his servants the prophets." Prophets were at work in the Book of Genesis. In fact, one of the very first humans, Abel, was a prophet. (See Luke 11:50–51.) And prophets continued to do their work throughout every single book of the Scriptures. All sixty-six books of the Bible testify to the activity of prophets, the presence of prophets, the ministry of prophets, and the words of prophets. Prophets are a vital part of God's plan. It has always been this way!

Yet people called to the office of a prophet are under assault today, either by bad doctrine, rebellion, character flaws, perversion, or environments that don't welcome them. They settle into ministries that ignore, overlook, or even worse, convince them that modern-day prophets do not exist.

This book gives ammunition and courage to people who have a true prophetic calling but who have been muzzled and held back in that calling. It gives strength to those God has called to be used in the prophetic and who have been criticized and ridiculed because of it. If that describes you, I want to motivate you to come out of hiding and become one with your calling. We need you!

PROPHETS ARE BORN

At this juncture in the world and in our scriptural history, we know that prophets are born. Please read this carefully: You cannot decide to become a prophet. You cannot wake up one day and decide you are going to call yourself "Prophet So-and-So." So many people change their titles based on trends. But that is not how the prophetic ministry works.

It is vital that you understand that prophets are born. They are born, and they are just as needed in the body of Christ and in the world as pastors, teachers, and evangelists. Yet somehow in our approach to Christianity we have come to believe that pastors, teachers, and evangelists are healthier or more needful ministries in the body. Unfortunately that is a massive deception that has been masterfully woven into many segments of Christianity.

Neglecting the ministry of the prophet is dangerous. If we do not welcome or have a place for the prophets among us, we willingly give the powers of hell our future. Yes, I said that!

Real, authentic prophets are needed in this time, not just for the sake of the church but for the sake of the world.

We are in need of prophets. We are in need of men and women who know they've been called to be prophets, who have been educated in their prophetic career, and who have submitted to the office of the prophetic and have conformed their entire lives to God's prophetic objectives. We need people who don't make up their own prophetic agenda but would rather fulfill the mission and mandate their biblical predecessors carried out in Scripture.

Yet for those who are called to the prophetic, that is a challenging thing to do. And that is because many churches don't have educational academies or tangible responsibilities for prophets. This causes those who are prophets to end up becoming rebels or ruining structures, even when they are trying to help. The prophets need a space to learn, grow, and operate in their calling!

If prophets do no more than what they are known for doing today—predicting houses, cars, and marriages—then we are going to lose yet another generation to cheap prophetic activity.

Here is the point I'm trying to make: Prophets are a necessity. Real prophets, authentic prophets, born prophets are needed in this time, not just for the sake of the church but for the sake of the world. God requires prophetic things to be said to acquaint people and nations with His agenda, His personality, His character, His logic, the way He thinks, and what He wants to do with them. In order to do that, He needs mouthpieces—vessels—that literally speak on behalf of Him, the invisible God. That is what prophets do. They prophesy on behalf of God!

If God required prophets in the biblical past to speak forth His agenda, it surely will take prophets now and in the future to do it too. But if prophets do no more than what they are known for doing today—predicting houses, cars, and marriages—then we are going to lose yet another generation to cheap prophetic activity.

We need more men and women of God who are less interested in being pretty and marketable and more interested in being credible, accurate, and professional in their prophetic services. If men and women who are committed to the call of the prophetic do not rise up, we are going to lose a whole generation to the perverse agenda that is coming aggressively at America. We need prophets, and we need prophets to behave as such!

BECOME WHO YOU ARE

My heart is grieved by the number of prophets who are running around behaving as evangelists or pastors. That is not a knock on those offices at all. It just means that prophets should behave as prophets.

It's like if a business executive tried to build a house. Construction is not his expertise! We need prophets to flow in their expertise rather than trying to be carbon copies of what they see. They see pastors and evangelists, so that is what they emulate. They are trying to be everything but what they are, and that does not please God at all. I want all prophets out there to remember that God is going to hold you accountable to what He called you to do. Prophets are change agents. We need to see them act in their office. They cannot sit back, watch the world die, and do nothing!

A lot of prophets have subjected their destinies to environments that are dedicated to convincing them that they should not exist, they have nothing to contribute to the ministry, and others are more valuable than they are. This is completely untrue! Ephesians 2:20 tells us the church was built on the foundation of the apostles and the prophets. Yet so many other ministries give more input into the local church than the ministries that actually founded it. We have evolved into a disjointed body because the founders have been buried. The founders and the power within the founding ministries have been concealed, mainly by bad teaching and bad leadership.

Prophets have also developed a bad rap. I believe this has happened due to a lack of education. Prophets have not been trained in the prophetic, and that has caused disastrous results. If a sixteen-year-old wakes up one morning and decides he wants to be a doctor, we don't tell that sixteen-year-old, "OK, go ahead and find someone to operate on." That is not how it works! Nobody looks at somebody who says he plans to be a dentist and says, "All right, fine. Go and find somebody to perform a root canal on." Yet in the church too often we say, "Oh, you're a prophet? What's the word of the Lord?" We expect a prophet to know how to prophesy right away without any training.

Prophets need training. That's the bottom line. In fact, the last thing someone being trained in the prophetic should do is prophesy. When I train my prophets, the last thing I have them do is prophesy. What they do first is learn.

If you are a prophet, the world does not simply need your skill or gift. It also needs you to be knowledge-able and educated in what you are doing. It needs you to have gone through rigorous training. It needs for you to have been corrected. It needs for you to have been tested. Just as doctors learn before they perform any test or administer any diagnosis, you too need to first learn about the work God has called you to do as a prophet. Just because you do something naturally does not mean you do it excellently.

If men and women who are committed to the call of the prophetic do not rise up, we are going to lose a whole generation to the perverse agenda that is coming aggressively at America.

Do you want to know how important this education piece is to God? One of the first schools on earth was founded and populated by prophets. Yes, that's right. The Bible speaks of companies of prophets, which many understand to be schools established by a prophet and filled with other prophets. (See 1 Samuel 19:18–24; 1 Kings 20:35; 2 Kings 2:3–15; 4:38.) Knowing this, it is inaccurate and a shame for people to say today's prophets do not need to be schooled. Prophets need training!

I believe there are many rogue and rebellious prophets out there because they long for training. They long for education. They long for someone to help them understand why they are the way they are, why they experience the things they experience, and why they feel what they feel. I have known of many prophets who ended up in mental health facilities because they didn't have anyone to educate them about their prophetic gift. They never found clarity and understanding about who they were, and it literally drove them crazy! It is unfortunate that the entire Bible was given to the world "by inspiration of God" (2 Tim. 3:16), meaning it was given prophetically, and yet so much of the church fights prophets' right to exist.

If you are a prophet, the world does not simply need your skill or gift. It also needs you to be knowledgeable and educated in what you are doing.

Now, I'm pretty sure many people reading this will say there are a lot of fake prophets out there. And they would be right! But there are just as many (if not more) fake pastors, fake teachers, and fake apostles. They just don't get the same criticism or the same scrutiny that prophets do.

Even so, prophets should not be discouraged. The more you understand the rich history behind the prophetic, the more you will understand why it is necessary for us to go through what we go through. Again, we were the first ministry demonstrated on the earth, as Luke 11:50–51 tells us Abel was a prophet. This means prophets have literally been around since the beginning.

If we were the first ministry, we should not be treated as if we are the least necessary. We predate half of the ministries people are engaged in today. Prophets were needed long before evangelists, pastors, or teachers were needed. Yet in today's normal church setting all of those offices are given more rank, more input, and more authority than the prophets. This should not be.

It must grieve the heart of God that so many in the church see the one ministry strictly dedicated to communicating His word and His thoughts, His voice and His sentences as optional. For example, no church would argue that evangelism is an obligation. Everybody thinks that. The same is true of prayer. Every church is going to believe that prayer is a responsibility and a duty. But few churches think that about the prophetic. To be a Christian and not believe in the prophetic is not an option. If you're going to be a Christian, you need to believe in and enthusiastically support the prophetic. It's an obligation.

WE ARE A PROPHET-LESS PEOPLE

We are living in a time when most churches, most cities, most regions, and most nations are prophet-less. Psalm 74:9 describes the condition of a prophet-less people when it says, "We no longer see your miraculous signs. All the prophets are gone, and no one can tell us when it will end" (NLT). You see, in the Old Testament world, people did not know where to go or what to do without prophets. People found out what God was saying and doing in their day through the prophets. In Psalm 74:9 we learn what happens when the prophets leave. Prophets are vital!

The unfortunate truth is that although we have this knowledge of the importance of prophets, we still struggle with prophets being mistreated and mishandled today. We struggle with churches and leaders who disrespect the office and authority of the prophet. We have been taught to receive from teachers, we have been taught to receive from pastors, and we have been taught to receive from deacons. We have been taught to receive from everybody but the prophets. There should not be such a thing as a church without at least two or three prophets who have active input in their environment. There is no way a church, ministry, or denomination can be future focused without the literal ministry of the future, the prophetic.

We need a course correction on the power of prophets and where they have gone and how the church cannot thrive without them. We need the church to understand how vital they are. But we also need every prophet to understand how vital they are.

That is what this book aims to do. It teaches you how vital the prophetic is and what it means to be responsible to the prophetic call. It teaches prophetic people how to see themselves and how to think differently about themselves, and it teaches the church why we need the prophetic to thrive for both the health of the church and the life of the world.

Sometimes when people write about the prophetic, they bring the essence of their theological stream to it. That could be a part of what is really hindering the potency of the prophetic today, because whenever you become the spokesperson of any one particular move of God, you really cease to speak for God.

If you're going to be a Christian, you need to believe in and enthusiastically support the prophetic. It's an obligation.

Additionally, attempts to pragmatize the prophetic and make it something people can reach for have diluted it…a lot. If we try to make the prophetic too easy, and if we compromise it in doing so, it loses the power to transform. It loses the power to change. The prophet's office requires our conformity, not the other way around.

I do not believe in making the prophet's office fit a particular person. Prophets need to be thrown into this ministry and to adapt to all that it is. Accordingly, prophetic writing should be challenging, and prophetic understanding should be challenging. As you try to understand it, it changes you as a person.

A lot of our contemporary application of the prophet's role on the earth is limited. We have trapped prophets into a 1 Corinthians 12–14 understanding of their role, but it is much broader than that. It sweeps across the entirety of Scripture! Millions of prophets around the world are trapped in edification, exhortation, and comfort. We've been taking that approach to the prophetic since Pentecost and the Latter Rain movement. We are well acquainted with those realms of the prophetic ministry, but we are missing out on the deeper functions of the prophet that nations relied on.

You can't convince me that Israel, Judah, or the inhabitants of Judea prospered from edification, exhortation, and comfort. The prophetic was so much more than that for them. The Old Testament world automatically traced any current problem to some form of idolatry. Also, in that world, the prophetic office had no solidarity. That is why Samuel's ministry was so relevant. What he did was clean the prophetic office out so that it would be seen exclusively as Jehovah's resource.

You cannot maturely train a prophet by simplifying the office of the prophet. Nothing else in life is simplified for them.

These are words that you rarely hear when you study the prophetic. You don't usually hear the term *duty*. You don't hear the term *obligation*. You don't hear the term *responsibility*. What do you hear? *Inspiration. Revelation. Utterance.* All of those things suggest that the role is under the will of a person or in the ownership of a person. This is why we are still in a twenty-year discussion on the differences between a *gift* and an *office*. The major difference is that a gift is in your control. It is not a lifestyle. But when you are called to an office and official status, you cease to have rights to civilian life. That's why a prophet will never be able to get away with what other people get away with or live any kind of way.

COME OUT, COME OUT, WHEREVER YOU ARE

Every day, due to neglect and the absence of education, we see more and more prophets go into their caves and into hiding. They don't feel respected, understood, appreciated, or loved. *That's* where all the prophets have gone—into hiding, just like those Obadiah hid from Jezebel in 1 Kings 18! Many prophets hide because the thing that was meant to protect them, cultivate them, and sharpen them has actually been killing them.

Prophets are the ones responsible for giving us what we know about the personality of God, the plans of God, and the purposes of God. In order to establish God's house, God's move, God's plans, and God's purposes, we need His mouthpieces to tell us those things, and the prophets are His mouthpieces. They are vital.

We most definitely have an uphill climb ahead of us in order for prophets to receive the respect they deserve. But those of you who are prophets need to be accountable to what God called you to do and what God called you to be. You need to stop pretending you are everything other than what you are. You need to be a prophet!

Along with this, our local churches need to make a more concerted effort to adequately furnish the prophets of God and to teach them how to wear their spiritual outfitting. We need to commit to teaching them their place in the context of the local church and, even beyond that, in the world today. We need all of the fivefold ministries in operation, but we desperately need more prophets to begin to behave like prophets. It is both needful and necessary.

We would see so many improvements in
the reduction of darkness in this world if we
compelled the prophets to come out of hiding
by giving them a safe place to seek refuge.

So many lives have not turned. So many destinies have not been redeemed. So many curses have not been broken. So many possibilities have not opened up. All this because the prophets of God are OK going to churches that don't prophesy and that don't welcome the prophetic anointing.

We would see so many improvements in the reduction of darkness in this world if we compelled the prophets to come out of hiding by giving them a safe place to seek refuge. The world depends on it! So much remains in darkness and in secret and at bay because the light ministries are not active.

From abuse to miseducation to ridicule, prophets have experienced so much. They do not need to be shut down, exiled, talked about, or exposed. They need to be trained, equipped, loved, educated, and steered. They need experienced, sober, submitted prophets to come into their lives and help build them up. They need to build relationships with other prophets so they can see they are not alone in the battle. They need to be given the freedom and access to grow. They need to be respected!

I know you may believe my opinion is biased because I am a prophet. And it is. But along with that, I have had the privilege of years and years of seeing the benefits of prophetic ministry and the office of the prophet. I have seen how the prophetic has literally saved lives. I know of prophets who have foreseen dangerous events happening and who have been able to do something to prevent harm. I have seen the prophetic pull people out of abusive relationships. I have seen the prophetic give hope to people who thought they had no more to give.

This is why the prophetic is so necessary. It's not so you can know a new car is coming or a house is in your future or a spouse is on the way. The prophetic is God's way of letting you know there is hope, you do have a future, and there is a way out! If that doesn't energize and excite you, then I don't know what will.

So where have all the prophets gone? Many prophets out there don't know what to do with themselves, so they stay away from the church. Then there are those who have found a church and a leader they like, one who makes them feel good, so they just ignore the thing that is literally leaping inside them. There are those who have a desire to pursue the prophetic but don't know how to educate themselves, so they just do what they've seen or what they think is right. They don't know how to apply themselves to the spiritual technologies in use regularly in their lives, and they get frustrated. They think they're beyond the church. They think they're beyond their community. They think they're beyond everyone else. But this is the furthest thing from the truth. Feeling misunderstood is what leads our prophets into hiding and away from where they need to be, which is in the church.

The prophetic is God's way of letting you know there is hope, you do have a future, and there is a way out!

If you are a runaway prophet in hiding, *we need you.* Your church needs you. Your family needs you. The world needs you. Everyone needs a prophet in his or her life. It's how God helps us handle and steward our deliverance. It is how God shows us where we need to go. The prophets of the world have gone into hiding, but it is long past time that they come out of the cave. The world is waiting!

PART I

THE FOUNDATION
OF A PROPHET

CHAPTER 1

The Prophetic Promise

To fully grasp the prophetic responsibility, we must first understand the prophetic promise. When I speak of this prophetic promise, I am referring to what God has always intended—and still intends—prophets to offer the world. I'm referring to what you can know, beyond a shadow of a doubt, God intended the prophetic office to be like.

We're going to learn this by looking at the story of Moses. The first thing we learn about the prophetic promise from the life of Moses is that it begins with relationship.

Moses encountered God in the burning bush in Exodus 3, and that encounter changed everything. Up to that point Moses was hiding out in the countryside, just tending his sheep, because he was afraid of what would happen if he came out of hiding. The last time he was out in public, bad things happened. He killed an Egyptian man he saw harassing a Hebrew man, and then two Hebrews turned on him for doing it.

Moses, whose dual citizenship rendered him an Egyptian (because he grew up in the pharaoh's house) and a Hebrew (because he was originally born to a Hebrew woman), fled. He was basically spending his days hiding out, just keeping his flock and himself safe.

But then Moses encountered the burning bush, and God said to him, "You're going to be the spokesperson for My people, and you're going to get Pharaoh to let My people go."

To be a prophet means you speak to others on God's behalf.

Now, Moses had a reaction to this. For a good many verses he went back and forth with God about this plan. "Who will I tell them sent me? And what about my stutter? And what if Your people don't listen to me?" But in the end he followed God's instructions. He decided the power that consumed the bush was greater than his fear of Pharaoh and the Hebrew people's disdain.

A NEW RELATIONSHIP

Now, all of this was extraordinary at the time because it meant the opening of a new relationship between God and the Hebrew people. Their situation was not like ours. We have years of writing and research to teach us about God and our faith history. They had none of those things. After all, Bible scholars have for centuries believed Moses was the human author of the first five books of the Old Testament.

That's why when God revealed Himself to Moses that first time, Moses asked, "Who am I going to tell them sent me?" And God introduced Himself, saying, "Tell them 'I AM THAT I AM'" (Exod. 3:14). God did two things here. He initiated a relationship with the Hebrew people, and He did it by activating a spokesperson. In that moment at the burning bush Moses gained official spokesperson status, becoming the person who would speak to Israel on God's behalf.

This is what it means, by the way, to be a prophet. It means you speak to others on God's behalf.

Now just imagine how a nation would respond to the introduction of such a spokesperson. The birth of the prophetic on such a scale was revolutionary at that time. First of all, if there were any gods among them, they hadn't been talking. Second of all, if those gods were to talk, they weren't expected to use an ordinary human channel to do so. But now God had given this ordinary, human spokesperson a message for the king of the known world—a call to deliver the ones He called His people, the Hebrews.

Objectively speaking, Pharaoh's response to Moses was natural. He had seen displays of supernatural power from sources other than the God of Israel. That's why when Moses cast down his rod in Exodus 7 and it became a snake, Pharaoh called in his magicians to do the same—and they did (vv. 8–12). This proves there wasn't an absence of supernatural power or paranormal activity at the time. That wasn't the overwhelmingly different thing God did through Moses.

No, what God did that wasn't being done was lead a whole group of people through the mouthpiece of one person. And He did it with extraordinary signs and wonders—probably to convince the Hebrew people to listen to Moses, believe what he said, and follow him.

Moses had to be a superb prophetic resource. He had to be an above-average communicator of information. Signs needed to follow him, and other massive, demonstrative things had to accompany his prophetic words to keep the Hebrews' focus on the right God. If Moses had not been that type of iconic prophetic resource, the Hebrews could easily have fallen into whatever those magicians were tapping into or whatever someone else made available.

I wanted to paint that picture so you would have some context for the rebellion or the indifference the Hebrews often showed to God or Moses along their journey to the Promised Land. Their rebellion was probably a natural response, given that even if they knew about the God of Abraham, Isaac, and Jacob, they had been enslaved for four hundred years and hadn't seen Him intervene. Add to that the fact that He chose to use Moses, a man many of them had seen grow up in Pharaoh's house, to present them with a promise of freedom.

Since the beginning of time the prophetic and the promise have always been related.

For even more context, keep in mind that when the Israelites were wandering in the wilderness, they were an infantile nation still getting used to knowing this God. A lot of times we criticize the Hebrews without understanding that walking with God was fresh and new to them. Even as God's spokesperson, Moses was still getting acquainted with Him. After all, he had only met God back in Exodus 3, when he asked, "Who will I say sent me?" He literally had to be introduced to the God of his assignment. Given these circumstances, you can see how trying to keep a whole nation under the auspices and leadership of God required the prophetic ministry.

THE PROPHETIC AND
THE PROMISE

This brings us to a powerful truth: since the beginning of time the prophetic and the promise have always been related. In fact, unless the prophetic is alive and active and consistent, people have no clue there are promises to live for or live up to.

In this case, God told Moses:

> Wherefore say unto the children of Israel, I am the LORD, and I will bring you out from under the burdens of the Egyptians, and I will rid you out of their bondage, and I will redeem you with a stretched out arm, and with great judgments:
>
> And I will take you to me for a people, and I will be to you a God: and ye shall know that I am the LORD your God, which bringeth you out from under the burdens of the Egyptians.
>
> And I will bring you in unto the land, concerning the which I did swear to give it to Abraham, to Isaac, and to Jacob; and I will give it you for an heritage: I am the LORD.
>
> —EXODUS 6:6–8

That's a promise. After they came out of slavery and the wilderness saga ensued, God started describing the land He would give them as a land flowing with milk and honey. (See Exodus 3:8.) He told them what He wanted for their ancestors and all the things they would get as a by-product of not only their obedience but also their solidarity, their fidelity, and their focus on the God of Abraham, Isaac, and Jacob. (See Exodus 23:20–33 and Deuteronomy 8.) All of this, too, was a promise.

Here's another point to consider that brings a lot of relevance to the prophetic in our contemporary context. It is always very risky to watch a people—or in this context, a nation—go through deliverance without a destination. The prophetic is that space between deliverance and destination. Everybody knows and understands that God wanted His people out. He always wants a people out! It's just that without the prophetic, they wrestle to know what they are to do with freedom once they have it, what to do after the victory has been won.

Moses must have spent days in prophecy. The only substantial way to keep people out of what they've come from is to have a vision for the future. Nobody stays out of the past without revelation of the future. And so, to keep the heart of the Hebrews in a willing spot to continue walking through wilderness to the Promised Land for all the time it took, Moses had to continue to feed them information about what their life over there was going to look like. All of that information? That's prophecy.

It is always very risky to watch a people go through deliverance without a destination.

I believe that once Moses got the Hebrews through the Red Sea, he spent time prophesying. And rightfully so—Moses was a prophet of God.

A NEW SYSTEM

After the exodus—after that whole dramatized scenario of crossing the nation over the Red Sea and killing Pharaoh's horsemen—the prophetic work continued. And that's because now there was a system in place. Moses had established himself in that culture and in that nation as the spokesperson for God, so much so that the people were coming to him asking for the word of the Lord.

Nobody stays out of the past without revelation of the future.

Now, when you're getting to know a new God who is claiming to be the God of all gods, you need to know a few things about Him:

- What offends Him

- How to be on His side

- How to invoke Him in times of need

- His plan for your future

All of these things made Moses' function so necessary. Once again, keep in mind that there was no Bible during this time. There were no elongated Pauline epistles. All they had was Moses' history with God and the messages God gave him to share with them. That's how the Hebrews built their entire civilization.

The prophetic even set up the moral code of the whole human race, as it was the prophetic, through Moses, that gave us the Ten Commandments. From then until now, entire nations have been set up on the laws that were revealed to Moses in a conversation on a mountain.

And then the Hebrew nation continued to grow. The Bible says the Hebrew women were "vigorous" and gave birth quickly (Exod. 1:19, AMP). They were strong, and they multiplied greatly.

All of this put a lot of pressure on Moses! From a purely numerical standpoint, he, as a lone person, could never have sufficiently supplied the nation with all the information they needed to set up their lives. One person could never have been responsible for handling all the conflicts, speaking to all the futures, or interpreting all the dreams and visions God gave them.

AN EVEN NEWER SYSTEM

That brings us to Numbers 11.

In Numbers 11 we see that Moses eventually became grieved that he had no one to help him manage the people. Now, Moses was not simply talking in a civil sense regarding the help he needed. He was also talking about those who were skilled in the prophetic. I say this right up front because a lot of people think Numbers 11 demonstrates a social or civil cry of Moses, where he was saying, "Help me judge the matter of the people!" But that was not the case.

We think God gave the seventy elders an ability to manage the legal and civic affairs of the nation, and we think that largely because of the way we approach the

Scriptures. We approach them too quickly. We don't really evaluate what they say. We read them through American eyes or our denominational context, and we want the Scriptures to mean what we've been taught. For most people this is second nature! They know no other way to look at the Scriptures. But what we begin to see is that very often the Scriptures mean the opposite of what is implied, particularly when you've been reading, studying, or preaching it with a hidden agenda or personal attachment.

In fact, what God did here was impart the prophetic spirit to seventy elders. That is how He brought relief to Moses—and spread the prophetic ministry even further too.

Look how the dialogue unfolds. Moses says:

> I am not able to bear all this people alone, because it is too heavy for me. And if thou deal thus with me, kill me, I pray thee, out of hand, if I have found favor in thy sight; and let me not see my wretchedness.
>
> —NUMBERS 11:14–15

And God replies:

> Gather unto me seventy men of the elders of Israel, whom thou knowest to be the elders of the people, and officers over them; and bring them unto the tabernacle of the congregation, that they may stand there with thee. And I will

come down and talk with thee there: and I will take of the spirit which is upon thee, and will put it upon them; and they shall bear the burden of the people with thee, that thou bear it not thyself alone.

—NUMBERS 11:16–17

Moses was facing a prophetic burden and responsibility. It was not a civil or social push. It was not a pastoral burden. Nor was it people management. It was God reinforcing the prophetic. He said, "I will take the same spirit that is on you and put it on them." God was talking about revelatory responsibility here; if the nation was to continue in momentum, they needed answers from God.

If Moses was talking about the people, he would have said, "They are too heavy for me," or, "This is too heavy for me." Instead he said, "It is too heavy for me." He was referring to the prophetic responsibility. He wasn't talking about leadership responsibility. He wasn't talking about handling the legal issues. The prophetic responsibility was the source by which people got to know their God—what He wanted, what He knew, what He was saying, His next actions, His mood, His temperament, His doings, His logic—all of that. The way God saw life. The way God saw the human race. His intention toward them.

God's perfect plan was known by the prophetic, and Moses was saying, "This is too much for me"—so much so that verse 15 says, "And if thou deal thus with me, kill me." Basically Moses was saying, "If this is the only way to continue to give them prophetic leadership, and if I am the only one who can do it, kill me."

And so in verse 16 God told Moses, "Gather unto me seventy men of the elders of Israel...and bring them unto the tabernacle of the congregation, that they may stand there with thee." I believe God was telling Moses here to gather men who could stand in the prophetic responsibility with him.

A PROPHETIC REVOLUTION

So what happened next? All the way down in verse 25, after the seventy elders had come to the tabernacle as instructed, we read:

> And the LORD came down in a cloud, and spake unto him, and took of the spirit that was upon him, and gave it unto the seventy elders: and it came to pass, that, when the spirit rested upon them, they prophesied, and did not cease.
>
> —NUMBERS 11:25

A legitimate prophetic revolution took place. Why? Because answers from heaven had been on back order. God had a lot to say, but with only one vessel to get through to thousands of people, only so much could be said. Now the seventy elders prophesied along with Moses, and there was no stopping that spirit on them.

And the LORD came down in a cloud, and spake unto him, and took of the spirit that was upon him, and gave it unto the seventy elders. —NUMBERS 11:25

One of the only other times we see something comparable to this is in the New Testament in Acts 2, when the people began to prophesy after the Holy Spirit came down on the day of Pentecost. Subsequently every time there was an outpouring of the Holy Ghost, people prophesied.

Part of what this shows us is the people who have been given the right to impart prophetic activity often see it as personal responsibility. And when someone entreats something as a matter of responsibility, they convey it differently.

We see, too, that the prophetic revolution extended beyond one physical place. The story continues:

> But there remained two of the men in the camp, the name of one was Eldad, and the name of the other Medad: and the spirit rested upon them; and they were of them that were written, but went not out unto the tabernacle: and they prophesied in the camp.
>
> —NUMBERS 11:26

We don't see Eldad and Medad being taught how to prophesy. They were outside of the tabernacle, so they couldn't have learned it through teaching or by observation. They couldn't have picked it up by second nature. The prophetic spirit simply came upon them and allowed them to prophesy.

A WARNING TO US

I am concerned that with each day we are seeing more and more of what we saw in Numbers 11—cities over-populated, potential wars, and answers from heaven on back order. I wonder if we would be the lights in the world we are called to be if we made the responsibility of the prophetic a foundation of our prophetic study and our prophetic training. But people don't see the prophetic as a responsibility. It's more of an afterthought. Think about what a disadvantage that puts people at, when divine communication becomes something negotiable.

God declares His mind and His heart through prophecy. He announces His agenda for humanity through His prophets. Through prophecy we discover His truth and His will. So how can we prosper if hearing the voice of God becomes an afterthought?

In Numbers 11, when God told Moses to call the seventy elders to come and stand with him in responsibility, God made a promise. He said, "I will come down and talk with thee there" (v. 17). That is so powerful. It shows that when people are willing to stand in their prophetic responsibility, God comes down. Moses' ability to bring people into seeing the prophetic as a responsibility provoked God to come down and have a degree of conversation that hadn't happened in quite that way before. And after God came down, He took of the spirit that was upon Moses and gave it to the seventy.

How can we prosper if hearing the voice of God becomes an afterthought?

Notice too that after God gave Moses the instructions about the seventy, His very next directive was for Moses to tell the people to sanctify themselves for tomorrow. (See Numbers 11:18.) I believe this points to the fact that the prophetic prepares us for tomorrow. If we don't do what we're supposed to do in our prophetic responsibility, then there's no way to be prepared for the future. It was always God's intent, for war's sake and for prosperity's sake, that people be prepared for tomorrow. But churches today are living as if the future has leadership over itself. This is not so. The prophetic burden on prophets is what prepares people for tomorrow.

Wherever there is human crisis, human indifference, or human indecision, the only thing that solves those issues are people who move in prophetic responsibility. It's different from singing or dancing. I think that's part of why the weight has left us. We treat the prophetic like it's something that accentuates Christian life, when in actuality the whole of the Christian life is founded upon prophecy.

Most of our Bible is prophecy. The whole of our interaction with God is prophetic in nature. We respond to Him as a result of the revelation of His divine will and purpose given to us through His Word, His servants, and His Spirit. I really believe it is a supernatural crime for the church to get to a place of thinking we can function effectively without God's voice and only rely on what He wrote. Our understanding of what He wrote comes from people who knew the spirit of the author! The prophetic spirit is the spirit that authored the Scriptures, which is why without prophets and prophetic people we're never going to be able to scratch half of the depth of the mysteries of God.

If we don't do what we're supposed to do in our prophetic responsibility, then there's no way to be prepared for the future. The prophetic burden on prophets is what prepares people for tomorrow.

If we could envision what the church universal would look like if hearing the voice of God were a priority, we'd know it would look a lot different from the way it does now. The prophetic has the ability to find the treasure in men. It has the ability to expose the enemy. It has the ability to solve human crime. It has the ability to locate lost things. It can also foretell events and geophysical disasters.

That's what made Elijah so dangerous. What he did when he shut the heavens in 1 Kings 17 reversed the entire economic status of their day. He made sure no one who owned land would reap a harvest. Even today people tell you the way to put on economic pressure is to not buy. They'll say, "Don't go to this store," or, "Don't support this business." Elijah did that as one man by saying it would not dew or rain except by his word.

I don't think that authority came as a matter of his personal decision. I think that level of authority flowed through him because he saw the prophetic as a responsibility. What consequences have come in the world because people were not being the prophets they needed to be? I don't think the church is halfway aware of what she is missing out on and the full scope of her assignment to the world.

Most of our attempts to reach the world are evangelistic in nature. We're reaching the intellect and not the heart. When you witness to a person, you have to witness to logic. You have to witness to education or to observation. You have to witness to training. You have to witness to willingness.

The prophetic is different. The recipient doesn't have to be willing. He or she doesn't have to be intelligent. The voice of the Lord is the only resource that can reach past a person's humanity and find the parts of him or her that are eternal. Our eternal selves can be reached by the voice of God. The spirit of the One who created us can speak directly to us. God knows how He created every human being on the planet, and He has something to say to everybody.

How absolutely illogical it is for the church to see the prophetic as an option! It is legitimately a matter of life and death. I believe not embracing the prophetic is why a lot of the church is bankrupt. It is why a lot of the genius God has invested in His people has gone untapped. I also believe it is why a lot of God's people end up exploring their potential dangerously and approaching the future flirtatiously. They just haphazardly and ignorantly decide what they believe God wants instead of seeking a revelation of His will. The prophetic is the only thing that secures the future before it arrives.

In an attempt to make the prophetic practical, we have highlighted the vocal aspects of it—the speaking forth of the word of the Lord. The prophetic does, indeed, communicate God's mind for the future. However, we need to press beyond that aspect into the interpretive needs of the prophetic. That is not just foretelling events as they're going to happen, but explaining what the events mean to humanity and to God. How are we to perform in them? All of that is prophetic in nature.

This is why every local church needs prophets. It's why anything that has to do with the kingdom of God must have prophets connected to it. I really don't believe we are going to see any harvest of souls without prophets and the prophetic. People have been prophesying a harvest of souls for years. I really believe one of the reasons we have not seen that harvest is because we don't have the resources to keep the people when they come.

God knows how He created every human being on the planet, and He has something to say to everybody.

If prophets are not in place, how are people going to be processed for the future? They won't be. They'll come and go. And they're going to backslide. If you don't give people a reason to live for the future, they return to the past they know. The prophetic is capable of doing that—of giving people a reason to live forward. It can speak to where a person has been and where a person is, and it can make tomorrow's answers known today. It is for this reason that we have to entreat the prophetic as a responsibility. It is not an option. It is not something that is the strength of certain moves or streams or any of that. The prophetic literally is a lifestyle that represents the interests of God, the opinions of God, the emotions of God, the doings of God, even the hand of God.

People normally treat all other aspects of the church as an obligation—things like prayer and worship and the reading of the Word. But those don't really give the type of contact God wants when it comes to reaching the lost or backslidden. If a backslidden person has a heart turned away from God, preaching may or may not reach him. Worship or music may or may not reach him. What makes that hand-to-hand combat with a life is the prophetic. It is personal.

The prophetic can speak to where a person has been and where a person is, and it can make tomorrow's answers known today.

That is another reason behind a lot of the perversion in today's church. With the way we portray Him, we're representing a God or talking for a God who has no personal interest in people. The way God shows His personal interest in people is through the prophetic. Evangelism is different from prophecy, because people can interpret evangelists as God's volunteers. But the prophetic is personal. It is God becoming personal with every human being He created and their purpose, their destiny, and their dangers. When the prophetic starts to reach, speak to, and clarify dangers that await someone, it is a very personal thing.

If we don't have the prophetic, we have no real way to pull people out of death, danger, disaster, and deception. Deception is the most powerful threat.

That's why we need to see the prophetic as a responsibility. It was always too heavy for one person to hold. The world needs prophets to be who they have been called to be. It needs them to accept their prophetic responsibility.

CHAPTER 2

The Prophetic Drought

W<small>HAT DOES A</small> society without communication from heaven look like? What do families without heavenly intel look like? What dangers does a society or nation get exposed to when this is the case?

Imagine where creation would be if there were no opportunity for God to speak. From our contemporary context, this may be hard to imagine. But picture Old Testament Israel. It existed inside a polytheistic culture, where new gods and worship rituals were being born every day. People gave themselves to whichever deity presented his or her agenda first, be it in sacrifice; in offerings; in blood covenants; or in civil, judicial, or military matters. Imagine what a complete absence of intel or foreknowledge from heaven would look like.

Here's how it would look. Everything that God's word and voice does would be absent. And if God's voice is absent, there is no creative power, there is no redemptive power, and there is no distinction in the realm of the spirit. Subsequently, certain agendas would have a right to everything. So it would look like people's inability to distinguish the will and the intent of anything in the spirit that has a voice—total confusion.

That is what a prophetic drought looks like.

AN INITIAL PICTURE

The Book of Amos describes it this way:

> "Behold, the days are coming," says the Lord God, "when I will send hunger over the land, not hunger for bread or a thirst for water, but rather [a hunger] for hearing the words of the Lord. People shall stagger from sea to sea [to the very ends of the earth] and from the north even to the east; they will roam here and there to seek the word of the Lord [longing for it as essential for life], but they will not find it."
> —Amos 8:11–12, amp

It is important to emphasize here, first of all, that these verses are not describing the absence of the word of the Lord. They are describing an absence of the *hearing* of the word of the Lord. And the consequence of such an era is described in verse 12, where people are staggering all over the place, roaming here and there to seek the word of God but being unable to find it. This is what it looks like when there is a prophetic drought, when there is a breach in communication between heaven and earth.

Prophets will always be necessary as long as the human race struggles to hear heaven clearly.

Now, it was never God's intention to halt His interaction with the human race. Relationships are strengthened by communication, and the prophetic in all of its manifestations is the medium by which God communicates with everything on the earth.

Prophets are God's timepieces. They are God's handlers. One way He invests Himself or expresses Himself is through prophets. Prophets are so necessary, and they will always be necessary as long as the human race struggles to hear heaven clearly. If the human race, for whatever reason, cannot readily hear God, then they cannot respond to the God they have not heard. Therefore, prophets have their place in perpetuity in God's plan for as long as there is earth. God is always going to want to broadcast and streamline His voice, thoughts, character, opinions, and actions, and He is always going to want to do this through the mouths of His prophets.

FARMING WISDOM

Amos was a farmer, and a lot of what God spoke to him had to do with fields, sheep, shepherds, and plowmen. God's use of that period—and His specific use of the word *drought* in the passage quoted previously—was related to Amos' experience. As someone who dealt with shepherds and herdsmen and the growth of a harvest and the process of the seasons, Amos knew firsthand what it was like to be in a drought. When God spoke of a drought to describe what it was like for the people to be unable to hear from heaven, Amos knew that would have been like death.

God is always going to want to broadcast and streamline His voice, thoughts, character, opinions, and actions, and He is always going to want to do this through the mouths of His prophets.

To a farmer, an agricultural person, or a herdsman, droughts are the absolute worst thing that can happen. They create economic loss. They bring about sickness and disease. When God said there would be a drought of people hearing from the Lord, He was describing civilization under a closed heaven. A closed heaven is akin to having no rain. The heavens being opened is a matter of all things health for human life. We are healed and restored, theoretically speaking, by what we eat and by the quality of our food, and all of that is determined by the level of rain that is received and the way things grow. Under a closed heaven—no rain— death happens.

Now, imagine a similar kind of life outside of the

mind and counsel of God. What's directing, validating, steering, convicting, turning, or aligning you if you have no access to God? To take it a step further, what would be drawing you? What would be pulling you? What would you seek after?

We know, on the other side of redemption, that God's voice initiates everything in the life of the believer. A person can't even come to the Lord unless He first draws them, and His first promptings in a person are the manifestation of His voice. So think about it. If you didn't have access to that, what would be persuading, pulling, drawing, or initiating you?

Amos helps us see what living under those conditions would be like. No access to an experience of God. No ability to explore His volume. Without a consistent release of God's voice, word, and will, it is virtually impossible to experience any of that. Life, health, and liberty are impossible without it.

THE STOP AND START OF GROWTH

Another reason the use of the term *drought* is significant here is because it shows, at least in the eyes of Amos, what is responsible for making things grow. He attributed growth to that which comes out of heaven, or he at least considered it necessary. The term *drought* signifies that in Amos' eyes, and probably in the eyes of many of his predecessors in Scripture, the word of the Lord is necessary for an earthly response. So if there is no heavenly initiation, then there can be no right response. But the human race was born to respond to God.

All growth is a right response to God. All progress is a right response to God. And if the heavens are closed, if there is a drought of the word of the Lord, then people have nothing to respond to. And if you have nothing to respond to, then you resort to the past or stay stagnant in the present. This is where sin cycles, addictions, bondages, and idolatry come from.

The drought is what happens when a culture gets entangled with the fetishes, fantasies, and festivals of the flesh. People's hearts get so entangled that they don't know what to do. This is what makes prophesying so powerful. A word from the Lord, from one vessel to another life, can settle the discussions and even the score. When a human heart has been directly confronted by the word of the Lord, there is no other reaction possible but rebellion or surrender. This is the bottom line.

Idolatry, though, is the human heart's attempt to find the future without the right God. Think about it. When people dedicated themselves to other gods in the Old Testament, they presented offerings to those gods in exchange for the gods putting their "blessing" on the area of that person's life that was most uncertain. If they could not bear children, they went to a fertility god and did whatever the god wanted so they could have a sense of luck or hope for their ability to bear children. If a businessman wanted the blessing of Baal, Ashtaroth, or some other deity, he presented offerings to that god and came into an agreement and covenant with whatever that god wanted. People went to those gods for their welfare and posterity. It was the hope of the human race that their livelihood would be sustained by the deity they aligned themselves with.

The human race was born to respond to God.

So you see, if there was a prophetic drought, if the heavens were closed and the Lord was not accessible, then who had the leverage in the affairs of human life? Those very consistent gods that were responsible for that Old Testament deity worship.

When the heavens close, the human heart wanders elsewhere. It is human nature to roam and wander. When a human life is not set apart or sanctified, then the seeking and searching heart that God put in every human being and intended for Himself gets steered in the direction of whatever promises success first. For this reason, a lot of people in destructive patterns, behaviors, or roles are in those places as a by-product of a mismanaged "seek." They seek after anything that is going to provide them a form of security.

Think about it. There are few things the human heart seeks more than security and success. Everything it ends up gravitating toward, whether in relationships or endeavors, is motivated by its search for security and success. Without God's word regularly thundering out of heaven, all of these other counsels, agendas, and patterns govern the human race. Without God and a regenerated human spirit, the human race is much more gullible and naïve than we can know.

When a human heart has been directly confronted by the word of the Lord, there is no other reaction possible but rebellion or surrender.

The forces of darkness are a part of this too. They are complex and know how to sway whole families and nations. Notice what happened when Daniel prayed. (See Daniel 10.) An angel eventually appeared and told him a prince was restricting communication between heaven and earth. That was why it took the angel so long to reach Daniel. He said, "I started coming in your direction the moment you started praying, but the prince of Persia withstood me until another angel came." (See Daniel 10:12–13.)

Let's consider what the prince of Persia was doing before Daniel began to pray for those answers. He was probably holding up answers. It was probably his second-heaven job to enforce the drought, in fact; if closing the heavens was not his motive, intent, and agenda, then he wouldn't have been able to restrict the response to Daniel's prayers. There was nothing the prince of Persia could do about Daniel's intercession. Daniel fasted and prayed all the time, but the answers were withstood by something that covered a whole nation: the prince of Persia.

Consider the implication of this story. It teaches us that it must be the agenda of certain demons to restrict revelation. Some of them must make it their whole intent to make sure certain generations or nations are not clear about what God wants to do.

And here's the thing. It could have been the prince of any family or the guardian of any city who did this. The point is that his terrain covered a whole nation. We know Daniel was able to permeate the blockage— but how many other people did that prince stop before Daniel? Daniel could not have been the only person praying in Babylon. I can't help but wonder how many people didn't know the answers to their prayers were being blocked by a force whose job it was to make sure the word of the Lord did not fall like rain. How many of them did not get answers?

A CITY WITHOUT RAIN

The word *drought* is rich for Amos to use for another reason. When he described what it was like when the word of the Lord went missing, he likened it to a city without rain. Now, when Jude criticized the prophets, he called them clouds without water. (See Jude 12.) They were carriers with no content and mouthpieces with no words. The word of the Lord is like rain, and rain is necessary for the continuation of all life. Nothing happens without rain. Nothing grows. Nothing rejuvenates. Nothing heals itself.

After a crop area has been parched, burned, or brought down by a natural disaster, nothing heals the earth like rain. And we have consistent examples of the word of the Lord being like water. The Bible talks about the washing of the water of the word (Eph. 5:26). Isaiah says the word of the Lord is like snow from heaven (Isa. 55:10–11), which is a form of rain. Moses too said, "Let my teaching fall like rain and my words descend like dew, like showers on new grass, like abundant rain on tender plants" (Deut. 32:2, NIV), referring yet again to the word of the Lord.

Even the precipitation cycle shows what the word of the Lord is like. Once the water leaves the ocean and comes back down in the form of dew or rain, it governs the growth of the entire planet. When the people of God saturate themselves with the word of the Lord, they grow, and the ministries and people connected to them can flourish. But when people don't have access to the word of the Lord, they are living literally in a dry land. In a dry land, everything goes: death, disease, disaster, chaos, and more of the same.

One of the greatest human crises in our generation is that people have vowed their allegiance to a God who they don't believe talks. It is a masterful demonic achievement, a brilliant thing to do, convincing people you can belong to a God who has nothing to say to you aside from His document. In order to interact with Him, you have to read the book He allowed men to write. Do you see how much that sounds like a punishment?

The human heart knows that the word of the Lord is alive. But if there is no access to that aliveness, then you are only the by-product of what you hear. If your heart, life, and world cannot hear it, the possibilities of having anything more are not there. You have to live your life according to cause and effect because the Lord has no opportunity to interject His word and His will into a circumstance or impending disaster.

The word of the Lord is like rain, and rain is necessary for the continuation of all life. Nothing happens without rain. Nothing grows. Nothing rejuvenates. Nothing heals itself.

Since the time of the Old Testament prophets God used His word, the word of the Lord, to progress the whole of a nation. But that is not so in our contemporary context. I believe the church is the platform of God. It is the threshold of God leading to the future.

One mistake we make when we explore the prophetic is that we often limit it to what we have seen in a local church. Because we have not broadened our investigation of the prophetic, the quality of what we bring to the church prophetically is also affected. Before the physical church was initiated, prophets were assigned to nations and neighborhoods. They were God's future source to those regions to which they had been assigned.

One of the greatest human crises in our generation is that people have vowed their allegiance to a God who they don't believe talks.

Just imagine what would happen to people who didn't think a future was possible. Anything could happen, because they wouldn't have anything to live for. Many people on death row do all kinds of monstrous things when they are in prison, because in their minds they're already paying a penalty that cannot be reversed. They're waiting on death. But the word of the Lord makes people live to wait on a future!

IT COMES THROUGH PROPHETS

Being able to bring people into the days that are yet to come and to announce to people what God has planned in the coming days focuses a heart for a clean pursuit. It focuses the decision-making skills of a human being for a clean pursuit. Jesus endured the cross "for the joy that was set before him" (Heb. 12:2)—that was the power of the prophets.

And this is why God chose that ministry, the

ministry of the prophets, as the conduit to get Jesus to the earth. He could have been promised by a priest, the way the story line went. He could have had priests hoping and believing a Messiah would come, having them just make offerings until He got here. But God chose, from the very beginning of the Book of Genesis, to use prophets to articulate to every generation, to prophesy, that the Messiah was coming.

I believe one of the reasons God did this is because offerings, which are in the purview of priests, do not give people hope. The priests might have been able to bring spiritual ideas to the people that a Messiah would come, but that would have done nothing for the people. An offering made by a priest doesn't necessarily give hope to the people who watch him give the offering.

But if people prophesy the Messiah? Write the Messiah? Even do like Isaiah did, which was to describe exactly what Messiah's processes were going to be? That brings hope! That makes it real!

The prophets prophesied the Messiah from generation to generation so that He would finally be made manifest and the drought would be forever ended. When Jesus got here, He said, "I am the living water." (See John 4:1–26.) That is why a prophet's chief ministry is the revelation of Jesus. All that we do and say is the manifestation of the Word incarnate. Revealing

Jesus is the objective of the prophets. He was the first ministry of the prophets.

AN OPEN HEAVEN

I love the geophysical manifestation that happened once Jesus came up from the water of baptism. Matthew 3:16 says "the heavens were opened." So an open heaven is the heritage of sons. What was God showing? He was using the heavens to declare what happens when a man obeys God.

A closed heaven, in contrast, is a response to disobedience. Obedience opens the heavens. But obedience to what? If there is no word, way, path, course, or predetermined story line to follow, what brings about the obedience? That is the basis of all of our prophesying.

We prophets don't just tap into the human spirit to figure out what to say to people. We have been given access to God's eternal writings on every human life, and a part of what we do is perceive and then broadcast something already published in eternity.

This has to be the case, because without a predetermined narrative for every life, it is impossible to see God's sovereignty. If there is no preset plan or purpose, then we are all making this up as we go along. But a part of what makes prophecy so powerful is that it utters forth heavenly documents over a life, heavenly decisions on a life—things that God was so confident about that He published these documents, had them written, signed them with His blood, put them in a library, and then revealed them to His prophets to say, "Read this!" Isn't that powerful? The word of the Lord for each individual life—unedited, unscathed, and unchanged!

God chose, from the very beginning of the Book of Genesis, to use prophets to articulate to every generation, to prophesy, that the Messiah was coming.

Now let's look at what happens when things move from a closed heaven to an open heaven. We find it in the ministry of the prophet Samuel. When Samuel was a young boy, hearing the word of the Lord was rare (1 Sam. 3:1). But the word of the Lord went from being rare to being multiplied during his lifetime—and it happened through the ministry of Samuel.

In 1 Samuel 3 we see Samuel serving the Lord in his early years. Then just a few chapters later we see he has a whole school full of prophets! (See 1 Samuel 19:18–24.) So whatever God put in Samuel ended the drought. It revolutionized the prophetic in that time. In 1 Samuel 10, when he is anointing Saul as king, Samuel tells Saul that a group of prophets will meet him at a certain time. He had to have some degree of confidence in those prophets to tell Saul to meet up with them. And if you are a veteran prophet, you are not going to refer novices to the future king! Samuel must have had some kind of relationship with those prophets. They must have been mature to some degree. That means the word of the Lord must have advanced during Samuel's life up to that point. It must have gone from being rare to being readily available. These multiple mouthpieces must have been comparable and capable in their duties if Samuel trusted them to address the next king!

All that was needed to end the drought was a life willing to surrender to the call of God.

Samuel was the opening. He brought about the end of the drought. What was on him was so powerful that the Scriptures say as long as he was alive, "the hand of the LORD was against the Philistines" (1 Sam. 7:13). All the man had to do was breathe and prophesy, and the Philistines couldn't prevail.

All that was needed to end the drought was a life willing to surrender to the call of God. I believe the end of the drought started when Samuel was boy, when he began putting his prophetic ministry in similar priority to his priestly service. His serving, worshipping, and responding the right way to the Lord showed how a life can stop a drought. He was responding to the Lord, and until he knew what to do, he kept going after God.

A lot of people stop going after God because they don't know what to do. But Samuel kept going to

God until he knew what God was saying. As a nine-year-old boy Samuel received from God the word for a nation. It was a word God could have given to Eli, but He didn't. He went past Eli to a nine-year-old boy. We should have known that the drought was over then!

When a nine-year-old got a word about a judgment and the edicts of God upon a nation, the water came on him immediately. The drought was over. How did it happen? Samuel demonstrated enough surrender to be trusted with the word of the Lord at that early age.

When the drought ended, new security measures were put in place. There were new border patrol systems intact. New surveillance over the nation. It happened through Samuel's life with the revival of the prophetic. One life kept God in opposition to a whole terrorist army. There was no drought there! Whatever Samuel was doing in abundance subdued that attack. After that, prophets began to be born and spiritually formed after the life of Samuel. And when he was done, Huldah emerged as a principal prophetess (2 Kings 22:14–20; 2 Chron. 34:22–28), and then we are introduced to the prophet Elijah.

The school of the prophets that came through Samuel was so important. God was able to consistently supply the world with people who saw the future and knew the "mysterion" of God, people who were taken into Him to see time and eternity and to be able to articulate and interpret things from the dream realm. Prophets are able to decode what happens in the dream realm because they are citizens of the space between time and eternity. They can manage the activity in both realms. We have to get the basis of our dream interpretation, and our sensitivity to them, from somewhere.

Ending droughts—that is part of what all prophets are called by God to do, whether that drought is in one life or family, over a whole nation or the world. If your word is to reverse the death campaign, you will need to have your graveyard tests. Every prophet has them. Can these dry bones live? I prophesied as I was commanded, and the subsequent activity was a response to that prophecy. So prophets, especially those in training, will always be put in dead situations and among dead things to see what they are going to do.

You are the water carrier. The water is the word. Open your mouth. That is how droughts change. Where there is a consistent prophet, harvests increase and seeds are planted all the time. Where there is consistent prophesying and the word of the Lord is streaming in a life, literally providing those life parameters and surveillances and boundaries that allow for healthy exploration and purposeful pursuit, then people can pursue the will of God. This is the ultimate reason we prophesy. We prophesy to keep people in the will of God. We prophesy to keep the drought at bay.

CHAPTER 3

The Prophetic Spirit

GOING BACK TO Numbers, we are reminded that part of God's promise to Moses was that He would take of the spirit that was on Moses and put it on the seventy:

> And the LORD said unto Moses, Gather unto me seventy men of the elders of Israel, whom thou knowest to be the elders of the people, and officers over them; and bring them unto the tabernacle of the congregation, that they may stand there with thee. And I will come down and talk with thee there: and I will take of the spirit which is upon thee, and will put it upon them; and they shall bear the burden of the people with thee, that thou bear it not thyself alone.
>
> —NUMBERS 11:16–17

In this chapter I want to talk about that spirit, which is the prophetic spirit.

The prophetic spirit is the unique spirit in all prophetic people that sensitizes them to the invisible world. It is a spirit given by God to everyone who has been called to the prophetic. This spirit gives them the sensitivities, proclivities, enablements, endowments, technologies, and capacities to adequately represent the God of heaven.

The prophetic spirit comes with features that make people uncannily open to the invisible world. They are not necessarily tapping into God's world, which I'll explain later, but they are open to the invisible realm nonetheless.

The prophetic spirit is the opening, or the access point, that makes a life a conduit of revelation.

The prophetic spirit is what was placed upon the seventy in Numbers 11, and it opened them up to the invisible world. But I believe it was their connection to Moses that caused them to direct the prophetic spirit they were given toward discerning the things of God. Remember, the people of Israel were still learning to follow God; they were still discovering how to relate to Him. Had the seventy had the prophetic spirit in them without a relationship with someone in whom the prophetic responsibility resided, someone who could guide them in how to use their gift, another deity could have gotten ahold of those abilities and spoken through those elders.

When the prophetic spirit is open in a person, that person needs to be committed to God, but I also believe that person needs to be connected to somebody who has prophetic responsibility to God. The prophetic spirit is like invisible hardware with features and sensitivities that are dangerous when unregulated. These abilities can be used by whatever the person is worshipping.

The prophetic spirit is the opening, or the access point, that makes a life a conduit of revelation. What determines if the prophet's revelation is from God is the vessel's loyalty to God. The prophetic spirit will speak for and amplify the opinions and thoughts of whatever being the person is in allegiance with.

When the seventy elders received the prophetic spirit, Moses was the one with the relationship with God. Because the seventy were connected to him, Moses was able to make sure they all spoke from the same source. The danger in the prophetic spirit being opened up in the lives of people who are not connected to somebody with prophetic responsibility is that the sources, the programs, and the agendas they represent will be mixed. They're going to have a mixed approach to spirituality because their supernatural skills are going to become accessible to whatever their hearts worship.

Again, I believe the seventy were able to speak for the God of Israel because they were being guided by

Moses. Had Moses been polytheistic, with a free-for-all approach to his spirituality, they would have been streaming information from diverse sources. This includes the gods of the land, the gods of the culture, the gods of the heavens, the gods of the waters, and the gods of any of the natural and the physical ornaments of their existence.

THE WIDE RANGE OF IT

Prophets don't just have intuition. Numbers 11 shows there is a prophetic spirit that comes upon a vessel. I have found that this means they are inclined to be sensitive to any activity, movement, action, reaction, and response in the invisible world. When prophets are born again and receive the regenerated spirit in Christ, it reawakens the prophetic spirit in them and makes them prone to prophesying for God.

Every true prophet prophesies. Whether it is for God is a decision of salvation. They're going to speak forth the mind of whatever is in front of them. Prophets usually make the best campaign staff. When prophets are in fraternities, they're often popular. When prophets are in business, they typically make the best salespeople. When prophets are a part of a gang, many times they're the ones the leaders send out first. This is due to their ability to amplify and to extend an agenda when they are a part of anything. This is why they tend to find themselves pushed to the top and the front of a thing. People often want to put them out there to be a spokesperson or the showcase because those with the prophetic spirit often have the capacity in their personality to effectively represent an organization or a cause.

Even if a prophet is usually quiet, when prophets are loud, they are loud. When they are drunken, they are loud. When they are under the arrest of a chemical, their real nature speaks up. They'll speak out in rage, or they'll speak out in an argument. All of those are capacities that are in the prophetic spirit. Even if those with a prophetic spirit don't speak up for themselves, the energy of that spirit will come out in debate, in defense of someone, or in clarifying a point when they are pushed in that way.

When a prophet decides to follow God, He cleanses his or her abilities. He then uses and employs the person for His service.

The prophetic spirit is, by nature, extreme. It is the opening and the vantage point through which any deity expresses its campaign or agenda. Therefore, it has to be extra-human. It has to be beyond human ability. That is one reason many unsanctified prophets will be intrinsically insulting or sarcastic. They have a quick wit and can discredit a point without spending much time thinking about it. Within them is that natural capacity to deflate an argument in order for truth to be known.

There is an improper cultivation of the prophetic spirit. The immature or demonic use of it is dangerous. An example is the ability, through the soul, to launch attacks at people for any reason. It can be used to impose judgments from a bitter heart or to achieve for selfish ambition or by selfish means. People with the prophetic spirit need to be Christlike and mentally and emotionally whole; if they're not, they will inevitably—and often inadvertently—inflict harm.

God expresses Himself in a myriad of ways. When a prophet decides to follow God, He cleanses his or her abilities. He then uses and employs the person for His service and the protection of the future.

All Christians may prophesy at one time or another, but the prophetic spirit is something God puts in those called to be prophets, and it gives them their abilities.

It must be noted that the prophetic spirit is different from the gift of prophecy. In his letter to the Corinthians, the apostle Paul wrote that he wished they all prophesied (1 Cor. 14:5). The gift of prophecy Paul referenced is an enabling of the Holy Spirit, but the prophetic spirit is given at birth, and it was present long before the Holy Spirit descended on the day of Pentecost.

All Christians may prophesy at one time or another, but the prophetic spirit is something God puts in those called to be prophets, and it gives them their abilities—it gives them their resources and skills. Those abilities grow over time as the prophet learns to cultivate them, take care of them, and protect them from dangerous exposure. Negligent teaching, sexual immorality, and cultural corruption can all decay and corrode the prophetic spirit, inciting prophets to do things they weren't meant to do.

EARLY EVIDENCE

People can notice they were born with the prophetic spirit, as it wakes up very early in life. As children they can tell. It can manifest as invisible friends. It can manifest as talking with themselves. It can manifest in a weird obsession with the supernatural or with mutants. Sometimes they have a bizarre fascination with the dead or with death, like fearing it or sensing that something is following them. It is that person's way of expressing that something about him is unlike other people.

Those with a prophetic spirit can be naturally poetic. They can easily make sense of things that don't make sense to other people. They are matter-of-fact because of the resources that are inside them. Those with a prophetic spirit have a profound ability to be decided; within them is the capacity to search for and investigate the truth.

First Corinthians 14:32 says, "And the spirit of the

prophets are subject to the prophets." I do not believe Paul was referencing the Holy Spirit here. I believe he was talking about the spirit that is native to every prophetic vessel who has accepted his or her responsibility. The spirit of the prophets is what makes a person a prophet. It's what creates a life for a prophetic calling or career. Either the prophetic spirit is there or it is not.

We see this in the story of Elijah and Elisha. The Bible says of the moment when Elijah departed, "The spirit of Elijah rests on Elisha" (2 Kings 2:15, NKJV). It was not talking about the Holy Spirit here, for the Holy Spirit had not yet fallen. It had to be talking about the prophet's ability. No one can identify the prophetic spirit like another prophet. As a result of his own history and experience, Elisha must have noticed that something different rested upon him.

When you have the prophetic spirit in you, you can call another person into your history with God. Elisha got called into Elijah's interactions with Israel's God, and that was the birthplace of his own ministry. That is how the spirit of the prophets was recognized and discerned by the prophets.

Something happened when the spirit of the prophet rested on Elisha. Interestingly the other prophets didn't recognize the spirit of the prophet until the mantle of the prophet fell upon Elisha. The spirit was probably already there, but it was not until after Elijah went up that the prophets saw that it was now resting on Elisha.

In our contemporary times there are a lot of people who are trying to wear one without the other. They want to walk in the prophet's mantle but don't have the prophetic spirit. But the prophet's mantle is no different from any other garment if the spirit is not in you. Either you are a prophet or you are not—no matter what you call yourself. If the prophetic spirit is not there, you will not have the ability of the prophet.

Today it is easy to mimic prophetic activity. But what determines whether the prophetic spirit is alive in a person is the response they get from the invisible world. Those with a prophetic spirit face harsh consequences when they rebel against their calling. The consequences are deeper, the timelines are shorter, and the margin for error is much narrower. A budding or emerging prophet often can be distinguished by how difficult life is, because the prophetic spirit has a built-in corrective resource. When a prophet goes too far, he often feels as if life is kicking back at him. This happens to get the prophet's attention.

But the prophet's mantle is no different from any other garment if the spirit is not in you. If the prophetic spirit is not there, you will not have the ability of the prophet.

It wasn't random that Jonah was swallowed by a big fish when he was thrown out of the boat due to his disobedience. That fish swallowed Jonah up to preserve his prophetic calling. It felt like disaster and danger to Jonah, but God kept Jonah alive in that environment. It was His plan to protect the prophetic spirit in Jonah.

THE SAME SPIRIT
IN MANY

Another feature of the prophetic spirit is covered in 1 Corinthians 14:29, which says, "Let two or three prophets speak, and let the others weigh what is said" (ESV). This means that by the time the third prophet spoke, the fourth and the fifth were probably brimming with eternal information.

This is the symbiotic nature of the prophetic spirit resident in all prophets. They can hear or sense the continuum of that word, or the point of that word, from God. They may or may not hear anything from God before the other prophets started talking.

It's a powerful tool, that the same spirit is in every prophet. A scenario common to a group of prophets in a ministry context is as follows: You're standing in line to give the word of the Lord to someone. After hearing the words given by the other prophets, you think, "Oh man, I had that too." How do all prophets have access to the same exact information without being in each other's minds? It's the same exact data source from heaven streaming to all of us, all the time, all around the world! It is what connects prophets universally—the prophetic spirit.

Societies need people with the prophetic spirit, because the human heart is very naïve. When a person is grieving, for example, the devil knows one of the easiest ways to turn a grieving heart toward his kingdom is to make the person believe that a medium has contacted a dead relative. If someone is suffering from the loss of a family member or dear friend, an easy way to cause deception is to profess to have heard from the dead. This is not from God; this is necromancy.

When you are feeling grief, loss, and devastation, you're often searching. You want to reconcile or say things you meant to say before. You may want to know how the person died or see if he is OK. Think about it. Satan takes advantage of people in this place, not only those who are grieving but also those who have the prophetic spirit, by making them think they're contacting the dead.

THE SPIRIT'S POWER

The prophetic spirit has an uncanny ability to reach the human heart without much effort or work. It can easily move past the soul to the core of a person. It gets instant contact to the heart. This is yet another reason Christianity needs prophets—because God uses the prophetic spirit in them to reach the heart of a person. The conviction power of the Holy Spirit will flow from the heart of God through the prophet and bring a person to repentance.

But when this spirit comes under attack in a society, Christianity loses some of its impact. People begin to keep God at arm's length because the voice of God in the earth is what helps people realize God has a plan and provision for their lives. The way, the route, and the story line a person is living, from the past into the future, requires direct contact with the divine, which flows through the prophetic spirit.

The devil spends so much time making prophets feel weird, they suppress the prophetic spirit inside them. They spend years feeling misunderstood, but it's a trap of the devil.

The church knows the spirit of prophecy, but I don't believe we have seen the full manifestation of the prophetic spirit yet. When a person is mature and she gives way to that spirit, she has abilities that far exceed her humanity. For instance, we have yet to see in our day prophets who could adequately deal with nature. We have not seen prophets speak to storms, tornadoes, thunder, or hailstorms and see them respond. We have not seen prophets close the heavens as Elijah did (1 Kings 17:1). We have not seen God send thunder and rain in response to the call of a prophet, as happened with Samuel (1 Sam. 12:17–18).

I believe this is because we have not seen prophets fully given over to the spirit in them. The devil spends so much time making prophets feel weird, they suppress the prophetic spirit inside them. They spend years feeling misunderstood because of this spirit within them, but it's a trap of the devil. He's endeavoring for them to never feel confident in who they are. But when people feel fully secure in their callings and release the prophetic spirit in themselves, it can do really unusual things.

The prophetic spirit usually gets stronger in times of moral, spiritual, and political unrest. God's word, spoken through the mouth of a prophetic vessel, has the power to settle affairs on that level. The oil of Elijah's spirit—the creative things he did to make intangible things materialize—was a manifestation and function of the prophetic spirit. It carries the ability to bless, to make alive, and to multiply. When a prophet is mature, he brings enrichment to his involvement in a thing. A mature prophet has the ability to make a thing better, enhancing its quality by refinement.

Survey some of what the prophetic spirit in Elijah accomplished: the miracle of the oil; the miracle of the rain; closing the heavens, and then reopening them by his prayers. Deep and resident within every prophet with this spirit made alive in them by God is the ability to change environments of any kind. The prophetic spirit is God's climate control, whether that be natural, spiritual, mental, emotional, or physiological.

This spirit has the ability to alter, arrange, reform, address, reduce, highlight, and uplift.

All of these are levels of the prophetic. And it is my position that the prophetic, in this day, has to become more than a "vocal" ministry, as Lester Sumrall classified the gift of prophecy in his book *The Gifts and Ministries of the Holy Spirit*. It has to demonstrate more power, not by volume but by altering and arranging things. We still have not seen the realm of prophetic judgments that I believe we're going to see. Judgments are a manifestation of righteousness. Prophetic judgments are also a by-product of the prophetic spirit.

When a man or woman can speak to an element in nature and it actually responds, that is a manifestation of the prophetic spirit present in those called to the office of a prophet. Moses stretched out his staff and opened the Red Sea. It was not his staff that split those waters. The parting of the waters was a manifestation of the prophetic spirit at work in his life.

The prophetic, in this day, has to demonstrate more power, not by volume but by altering and arranging things.

The prophetic spirit is what gives prophets the boldness they need in times of danger. They possess an abnormal fearlessness to say what other people think is inappropriate or what others will not say. When they are immature, prophets have to be taught to manage their tongues because they have within them the drive to say the unsaid and expose the hidden.

Think about how much truth has gone unsaid. Even more, what has gone unknown? This kind of revelation is channeled through a prophetic spirit and a prophetic voice. Think about how perfected and how mature God's people would be if they had regular access to that kind of revelation.

A SPIRIT THAT PERFECTS

It is impossible for the church to be perfected without prophets. The prophetic spirit is a maturing spirit. It is a spirit that helps to mature the body and graduate people into the deeper things of God. Without it there can be no progress.

The prophetic spirit active in a life surrendered to God brings about great power. In a life focused on prophetic responsibility, it makes great things possible.

I'm often amazed at how much authority is in the prophetic spirit. When Elisha healed Naaman of leprosy in 2 Kings 5, for example, he merely sent word by a messenger explaining what Naaman should do, which was to wash in the river Jordan seven times. His authority was so strong that he could send word through another person for a thing to be done to bring about healing, and the healing was granted. I've often wondered if Naaman would have been healed in another body of water had Elisha named a different river. Did God tell Elisha to say the Jordan River, or was that just the first river that came to Elisha's mind?

We see this with the prophet Samuel too. We are told God let none of Samuel's words fall to the ground (1 Sam. 3:19). It is as though God told Samuel, "If you say it, I will back it." It wasn't the ability to hear God perfectly that gave Samuel's words power; it was simply his saying them. People often treat it like God was saying to Samuel, "You will always get it right when you speak for Me." Rather, God sealed His approval on Samuel's words so they would not fall to the ground.

Imagine the maturity Samuel must have had to gain that type of commitment from God. But that is one of the discretionary powers of every prophet. You have the ability to bless and curse at will. We see this in the story of Balaam, too, where we're shown that he could muster the power from the prophetic spirit at will to reverse, to bring cursing upon, and to rail upon a thing. (See Numbers 22:1–21.)

Even in moments of discouragement, depression, and confusion a prophetic person has to be very careful of what she says, as the spirit will start to manifest the things around her to be in obedience to what is in her. If you as a prophetic person say, "My life isn't going right," you make that a part of your confession. The invisible world does not know you're only venting. And the more that becomes your decree, the more it begins to manifest. Creation is only doing its job by responding to the prophetic spirit. It may respond with things that were not meant to happen, but the prophet's negativity and lack of restraint licensed the manifestation of those things through the prophetic spirit in them.

The prophetic spirit helps to mature the body and graduate people into the deeper things of God.

Here's what I'm saying. You can prophesy your way into problems by not watching your mouth. We see this in the Book of Ecclesiastes, where angels carry out words. (See Ecclesiastes 5:6.) Heavenly angels do the bidding of the word of the Lord. Those of every nature, demonic and divine, wait for certain words to grant them permission to do their bidding. And some things manifest because of an unregulated prophetic spirit.

BLESSINGS AND CURSES

In a period when people are used to living under curses, God's answer is a prophetic spirit. It is equipped for times of emergency, crisis, and calamity.

Today there are so many people living cursed who don't know it. I think our civilization is full of curses. I'm not talking about profane words. I'm referring to binding word contracts, negative word statements, and designations that I'm convinced are mustered in the deepest places of hell to arrest lives and cause perversion.

A curse can work through a whole generation and linger. God's prophets can reverse the works of a curse by declaring blessing and by calling the word of God into manifestation. Certain things will remain jinxed until the word of the Lord comes to it. The answer to hell's decree over a thing is to reverse it.

What happens when prophets are silent? What is allowable? What manifests and what transpires in these instances? Without the prophets there is no way at all to monitor, to patrol, or to administrate invisible activity. Curses can and will occur. Hindrances and traps can happen. All types of spiritual crime are allowable if prophets don't speak up. That is the prophetic spirit and the powerful manifestation of God's word and will. It is the strength that fuels the prophetic spirit.

You can prophesy your way into problems by not watching your mouth.

It's so important that the prophetic spirit find healthy expression. Without it, we corrode culture. For those with the prophetic spirit, this is our obligation to a dying world. If you're a prophetic person, you should be burdened about prophesying. God didn't bring salvation just to keep people from hell; He saves us so we can live out His individual and customized purpose for our lives! That message is spoken, expressed through, and protected by the prophetic spirit.

Without the prophetic ministry, the church as a whole is going nowhere. The global church is in a cycle—moving but not progressing—because the future ministries have been under arrest. They don't know what to do with the prophetic spirit.

I already know the complaints: that the prophetic spirit is spontaneous, that it can mess up order, that it can get in the middle of things and disrupt them. Yes, the prophetic spirit can be disruptive. That is why another governing anointing is needed to help it find its context. And yes, sometimes a church or a life does merit disturbance. The prophetic ministry is meant to tear down what is built or erected incorrectly. That's why God put the prophetic at the foundation of the church; it disrupts to bring things back in alignment. And yes, sometimes stuff goes wrong when the prophetic spirit is active in a person, even when he or she is trying to help. This, too, is a manifestation of the prophetic spirit, as it is the prophet's nature to undo what was done inappropriately or inaccurately. The prophet has an undoing anointing.

Prophets are God's veto system. We legitimately carry within our mouths the power to reverse a series of events. We change fates and announce destiny. The prophetic spirit opens up lives and moves people into heavenly possibility. That is the power of the prophetic spirit.

CHAPTER 4

The Prophetic Responsibility

WHEN YOU THINK about prophetic issues, a broad spectrum of tag words come to mind, including *revelation*, *visions*, *dreams*, *sensing*, *discern*, and *activate*... a lot of descriptive terms.

One thing that doesn't come to mind, particularly when dealing with the ministry of the prophet and prophetic assignments, is the word *responsibility*. When a person realizes he has a prophetic call, what often surfaces in that heart is fear of responsibility, even if he doesn't know what being called to the prophetic really means.

The heart in its sin nature responds awkwardly to the possibility of responsibility. It takes a while for people to learn the depth of responsibility. I think this is true for all people but especially for those who are going to be stewards of God's voice. God uses prophets to make His plans known in the earth. Throughout Scripture, God used prophets to declare His will to kings and nations. He used prophets to declare judgment and correction to His people and ultimately to prepare them for the coming of the Messiah.

Responsibility is the right response to ability.

God still uses prophets as His mouthpieces today. They are still how He reveals His plans and purposes for individuals, churches, and even nations. Because prophets bear the responsibility of speaking forth the word of the Lord, they tend to fear the possibility of failure, especially prophetic people who have an unrenewed mind. There are prophets who are paralyzed by a fear of failure for years before they fully allow themselves to engage their calling.

There are people who gravitate toward their abilities in the prophetic. Many of them get good at their prophetic abilities—the sensations, the seeings, the praying, the knowing, even the counsel. But responsibility is the right response to ability.

God puts abilities in every person. You are born with abilities that make you a good, quality prophet. But your response and relationship to those traits—more than the traits themselves—are what make you a useful conduit of God's voice and God's word.

Responsibility has to become a massive part of

how we engage the prophetic so it is not treated as an afterthought or as something that enhances a special church service. There are so many things that God wants to manifest on the planet that cannot be revealed if we don't become capable of healthily receiving responsibility.

IT'S ABOUT AVAILABILITY

When you're dealing with prophetic responsibility, you are dealing with an assignment to allow God to do something *to* you and then *through* you. If you fear responsibility in a prophetic sense, it's because you place more confidence in your inability than your availability.

But responsibility is about availability. It is not about personal ability. In its very essence, being a prophet is about being a conduit. It's about being a channel. It's about allowing something to flow through your life. It's not about whether you get something right or wrong.

The only real threat is not being available enough— or not being present enough to remain available. When Satan wants to obstruct prophetic service, he hinders a prophetic vessel's availability. He hinders the prophet from being fully present in his or her calling. We see that prototypically in the life of Jonah. He ran away! In addition, I love how prophetic responsibility is outlined in Ezekiel. For several chapters beginning in chapter 2, God went back and forth with Ezekiel in dialogue about what he was to do.

If you look closely into how God talked to Ezekiel, you will see He often told him, "And sometimes they're not going to listen." The phrase is, "Whether they will hear, or whether they will forbear" (Ezek. 2:5, 7). He basically conditioned Ezekiel for what to expect. He was training him to be available and to not allow the reaction of his audience to determine the degree of his availability. Ezekiel would have dropped his responsibility without that training.

This is why God told him, "If you don't do this, if you don't work, if I can't make a sure sound through you, then the blood of the wicked I will require at your hand." (See Ezekiel 3:18, 20; 33:8.) It was God's way of convincing him to remain open, to allow God to say and do and be through him what He needed to be to that people.

A person can get in the way of his or her assignment, whether it be by fear or timidity or just not growing fully into that responsibility. The most challenging thing is to communicate truth with mixed availability. Jonah was just not available enough. He occupied himself with thoughts of what obeying his calling could mean, with his concerns about Nineveh, and with the other things that vied for his attention. All of that got in the way of his availability.

THE CONCERN OF TODAY

Today's contemporary prophetic movement seems to be about everything but responsibility. There is an over-emphasis on learning to prophesy well. What's almost sadistic about that is that you have people learning to prophesy before they learn the history of the prophetic. You have a lot of people who are coming into prophetic abilities and going to trainings and seminars, developing new abilities, but they don't have a context for the responsibility that they have now come into contact with.

---

*If you fear responsibility in a prophetic sense,
it's because you place more confidence
in your inability than your availability.*

The risk here is that ability is not always enough to keep you available. Just because you have the ability to prophesy or God opens up channels of communication to you does not mean the dealings of God are in you. You must have a consistent opening for God to manifest His word through you as His mouthpiece. That's responsibility.

I think God's primary desire for His prophets and anyone on a prophetic assignment is continually matured availability. Are you always living an available life? There are things that prevent prophets from being as available as they should be. Most of them involve the self; life experiences, people experiences, premonitions about failure in a career—all of these things preoccupy a person's availability. And a person can only be responsible to the degree to which he or she is available.

THE DEVIL'S INTENT

Satan, above all, is afraid of God's word. So it is Satan's desire to preoccupy people called to prophetic service with everything other than becoming an integral carrier of the mind of God. He will occupy them with the alleged testing that comes for prophets, or the sufferings that come for prophets. I even believe there is a degree of deception out there where Satan embellishes the possibility and threat of literally losing your life to your calling, all because Jesus said, "whoever loses his life for my sake will find it" (Matt. 10:39, ESV).

A person can only be responsible to the degree to which he or she is available.

A lot of people who have the prophetic ability won't say yes to a prophetic calling because they are afraid of what the devil will do to them, their kids, their body, or their house. A lot of people stay restricted from the prophetic ability for this reason.

I think it's a very strategic thing that Satan does here to keep people from yielding to that degree of responsibility. If nobody takes responsibility for what needs to be done, the events of history as we know it will go unchanged and repeat themselves.

What prophets and prophetic people do is take responsibility for events on the earth as they were preplanned in God's mind. We basically become the stewards who announce and broadcast God's plans for society and creation. And there is legitimately nothing on earth about which God does not have something to say. There must be revelatory regulation like dreams and discerning to measure a happening against the plan of God. We need to take action against anything that is happening, or that could happen, that would threaten or oppose something God has already planned.

THE RESPONSIBILITY IS GOD'S

Everything we do is based upon God's foreknowledge. It is not our responsibility to know what needs to be known. It is our responsibility to perceive and yield to what God has done. The scope and capacity of our words need to be based in Scripture and in our relationship with God as holy communicators. We can't be afraid of responsibility, or of the responsibility of our caucus.

All in all, the responsibility of the future is God's. He has planned it out, He has designed it, He has written it, and He has chronicled it. What we do is articulate what is written in the codes of eternity for every human life, for every human affair, and for every human event. We give expression to it.

That takes the pressure off your imperfection, doesn't it? The accuracy of your prophetic voice is not always about how perfect you are going to be as a human being; it's about the depth of your availability. The greater the depth of your availability, the more mature you become. Being available to God is what matures a prophetic vessel, because the word matures you as you carry it. That is why God told Ezekiel to feed his belly and fill his stomach with the scroll (Ezek. 3:3). The word matured him and did something to him physiologically that made him a compatible carrier of God's word.

When you are a legitimate prophet of God, you don't have to make up what to say. The stress of having to figure out, from your soul, what to say to people or what to say about a season is a distraction. All you have to do is yield to the Spirit that is in you that knows everything that needs to happen.

I can guarantee you that if God supplied the planet with thousands of prophets and 90 percent of them were not in active service, it would be because of their fear of responsibility. It's them saying, "I don't want that task." But the challenge is, what is our real task? The pressure of the events and the plans is not on us. The pressure is on us to say what we've heard and to declare what we've seen. If we learn how to say what we've heard and to declare what we've seen, then we don't have the pressure of being right or wrong. That is the example Micaiah gives us in 1 Kings 22 when he says, "As the LORD lives, whatever the LORD says to me, that I will speak" (v. 14, NKJV).

THE PROPHETIC GIMMICK

In America the prophetic gets a bad rap because people—prophetic people, even—have a tendency to say things God has not said. This has created a stigma around prophetic service and prophetic activity, which breaks God's heart.

When you are a legitimate prophet of God, you don't have to make up what to say. All you have to do is yield to the Spirit that is in you that knows everything that needs to happen.

If the whole of our planet was set up by the word of God, how ironic is it that this ministry has become attached to parlor tricks? There are more gimmicks around the prophetic than any other calling. You don't really see evangelistic gimmicks. Nobody's saying, "If you get saved, I'll give you prosperity handkerchiefs." We don't do that. You don't even see gimmicks surrounding the gift of teaching.

There are more gimmicks around the gifts of the Spirit and a prophetic calling than anything else. How masterful of Satan to make the people who are responsible for articulating God's mind and God's counsel in the earth parallel to mockery and jokes. It's been that way from the beginning of the Charismatic Renewal. There are so many gimmicks, primarily because the prophetic (unlike any other ministry except the apostolic) is directly connected to the economy and wealth. No other ministry gift has the ability to retrieve money like this. This is why prophets get crazy around offering time. Intrinsic to the voice of the Lord is the call to prosper. People abuse that, and the prophetic becomes a parlor trick. Novices, and even false prophets, tap into those resident powers of the prophet for their provisional needs.

If we learn how to say what we've heard God say and to declare what we've seen, then we don't have the pressure of being right or wrong.

Now, there is a stream of the prophetic that is strictly for provision, and it is not immature or elementary. People in the body of Christ and around the world war over provision, and the prophetic has the ability to open up God's supply. We see that with Elijah and the widow's oil. We see the ravens coming to supply Elijah at the river. There really is a realm of the prophetic that is provisional. But the devil has set it up so that power and skill in the prophetic has attracted the tricks, the salesman status, the jokes, and the gimmicks around it.

A lot of people who are legitimately called to the prophetic office shy away from it because of how highly abused this thing has become. We have an uphill climb, for sure, because the prophetic has experienced decades of degradation. Decades!

THE PERVERSION
OF TRUTH

Ultimately this is Satan's age-old mode of operations. He wants nothing more than for God to look like a liar. We see it all the way back in Genesis. The serpent said to Eve, "Go ahead and eat from that tree, because God knows that if you eat it, you will be like Him." (See Genesis 3:5.) But Adam and Eve were already like God (Gen. 1:26). Satan was the liar, but he made God out to be the liar instead.

The perversion of the truth is a powerful campaign of Satan. He wants to distort it and pervert it. He also does this through definitions. Satan will attack how people, even a whole generation of people, define things. Notice that the prophetic is God's *word* ministry. A part of what mature prophets who are available have the right to do is settle a definition in the earth. They're able to say, "This is what this means. This is what God calls it."

The prophetic ministry goes much deeper than giving advice. This thing influences the entire language of the human race as they know it, and how they see God. Without a prophetic channel people are left to try to figure out for themselves what God is saying. That's why they come up with their own gods. If people don't see trustworthy, reliable representatives of God, they come up with a version of Him they can live with instead.

Where there is no availability, there is no authority.

The prophets are the ones who articulate and express and represent the God that they know, firsthand. You can see how available God wanted the Bible prophets to be by the way He called them. Isaiah 6, when God allowed Isaiah to experience that call with the angels that commissioned him, was about availability.

When God called Jeremiah, He said, "I set you above nations, and you're going to root out and pull down." Jeremiah said, "I'm but a child." But God said, "Don't say that." (See Jeremiah 1:5–12.) I don't think God was ignoring the fact that what Jeremiah said was true. It's just that Jeremiah was using his youth as an excuse that got in the way of his availability. Where there is no availability, there is no authority. Think about what fear does; it makes you less available. It preoccupies you in your life, your language, your mouth, your approach, and even your responses.

AN AVAILABLE VESSEL

Persecution often makes a prophet more available. That is why God allows it. There is nothing like the peril of coming into contact with what you can't handle to create a hollow place in you for water to flow through. That is why God doesn't spare a prophet from persecution. He just preserves the prophet in the midst of it. It's as if God is saying, "I'll let you feel this and not let it kill you. I'll let you experience this and not let it overwhelm you. What I'm doing is creating an empty spot in you that only My purpose can fill and that only My word will satisfy." This is what Jesus meant when He said, "My will is to do the will of him that sent me." (See John 6:38.) He was an available man.

This is what set Daniel apart too. Think about it. When he displayed his mastery over the magi (Dan. 2:48), we have no proof of what they had been doing, but we have an idea because we saw what Daniel did. He lived a devoted life and kept a steady heart with fasting and prayer, probably cultivating availability. Now, there are people pressing into God for answers they can't tolerate. Prayer creates the toleration, the readiness for revelation that is beyond who you are, what you know, and what you did. Daniel's interpretation of that dream—that was not a google-able thing. The revelation was poured out because he had made himself available.

I think a picture of this is when the Bible said

Samson came to the place with "heaps upon heaps" and "with the jawbone of an ass" (Judg. 15:16). After he clave (or cut open) the jawbone, there was an empty space in it, and water flowed through the empty space. Additionally, Jesus said, "He that believeth on me, as the scripture hath said, out of his belly shall flow rivers of living water" (John 7:38). What are these pictures of? Cavities that are available.

When God starts to prepare a prophet for service, He goes to work on his or her availability for years. Every prophet of God will go through a phase of legitimate life reconfiguration. There are physiological enhancements that every prophet of God has to go through. Your time with God starts to become more than devotional; it becomes preparatory. The way you see things will change, the way you hear things will change, and even the way you remember things will change.

Prophets spend more time in preparation than they actually do in ministry because it takes a lifetime for them to become as available as God wants them to be.

When they become available, prophets start to remember unusual details about life. They remember things they could not naturally know. They'll remember their first experience with the voice of the Lord, even if it was not what they knew it to be. They'll remember the first time they felt the steel bit of the Holy Spirit and began to follow His promptings. And then God sanctifies it. He blows on it and uses it for His service.

Prophets spend more time in preparation than they actually do in ministry because it takes a lifetime for them to become as available as God wants them to be. You can rush to learn to operate in the prophetic and use the abilities God gave you. But having prophetic availability? That's something God has to change. It is not just saying, "Lord, do You have a word for this one or a word for that one? Here am I, send me." No, it's about making your life compatible to carry God's counsel unscathed, free from judgment, and free from opinion, handling it responsibly.

A YIELDED LIFE

I believe a lot of prophetic people would be liberated from fear of their assignments if they took the pressure off their personhood and just became yielded.

A prophetic life must be a totally yielded life, because carrying God's word brings with it the attraction of the spiritual realm. You get a lot of attention in the invisible world, which has the potential to do a lot to you. But if you master your availability, master your consistency, and master your ability, you will receive sensings and a range of revelation beyond anything you have ever been taught. That is the prophetic responsibility. It is not just my responsibility to prophesy; it is my responsibility to be available to the God I represent.

In my dedication to representing Him, I grow to know what He is saying to everything around me.

See, we have to reset our whole mindset and make it less about prophetic tactics and more about the prophetic life. We need to rearrange the prophetic mentality. The prophet's availability affects the quality, the content, and even the potency of a prophecy. When a prophetic person is still wrestling with being infatuated with his former life, when he is still living in some degree of regret about what he feels like his calling has made him miss out on, that mixture is going to be there when he conveys a message. That conduit has not completely resolved God's intent toward it. When he conveys God word to another person, it may be affected by that mixed, undecided, or unresolved lens. It is a dangerous thing to know the mind of God, the heart of God, the voice of God, and still be in competition over your availability. A preoccupied prophet is a compromised one.

A lot of prophetic people would be liberated from fear of their assignments if they took the pressure off their personhood and just became yielded.

That's the challenge. The word of the Lord, in its perfect state, has to flow through an imperfect person to achieve its task in another person. If we start to see ourselves as conduits who must live clear lives—Paul said he had a clear conscience (Acts 23:1)—then it takes the nervousness and the panic away from our prophesying and our prophetic service.

This is a powerful thing! It means that being prophetic is not about your perfection in your strength. God will perfect the one who is yielded to Him, and everything around you will go into His perfection for you. Good, bad, indifferent, ugly, now, later—it will all perfect you so that you can perfect what you do for Him. That is the prophetic responsibility.

A NECESSARY GIFT

The other part to this, though, is that the church needs to resolve itself to embrace this gift. Most of the church approaches the prophetic like it is optional, like it's a strength or a personality type. It's wrong to say things like, "Jesus is the answer," implying God has a plan, but then to go on and say, "We don't know how that's going to be known, so open the Scriptures and figure it out for yourself." That is so impersonal, and it is not our biblical heritage. Our biblical heritage is God arresting lives in a very personal way. It was always very direct.

Jesus Christ was personally aware of every life that would ever be born on the earth. Even if it were just for one human, He still would have shed His blood for that person. Prophets are facilitating a discussion between a fallen person and a holy God who knows that fallen person has the potential to be like Him.

We think personal prophecy is a cherry on top of the whipped cream, but it is the whole of our success as Christians—we need people with the ability to convey the word of the Lord.

People prosper in their purpose, but purpose is not figured out; it is revealed.

We have a revelatory obligation to a dying world—a priority to continually supply people and places with the voice of God and the word of God. It is an obligation. To be Christian and not embrace the prophetic should not be an option. How else are we meant to live our lives and direct our desires? How do we use our passions and accomplish what we are supposed to do without prophetic purposes? It will always be a gamble. And if purpose is a gamble, so is prosperity.

People prosper in their purpose, but purpose is not figured out; it is revealed. Whenever God wanted a man to make a geographic move, He revealed it by His word. If he wanted someone to start a business, He revealed it by His word. If He wanted a person to build something, He revealed it by His word. If He wanted to break a curse, He did it by his word. The same with a blessing; God opened up the blessing by His word.

Think about how many eternal initiatives must be stunted because God can't find a person available enough to take this responsibility. I think this is a profound loss. Given that communication gap, a lot can happen on the earth that is not God's will.

Who will take up the slack for that? It has to be God's prophets, God's prophetic counselors, and God's prophetic intercessors. Let us be part of God's work to bring this about.

PART II

THE MAKING
OF A PROPHET

CHAPTER 5

Open Eyes

PROPHETS ARE CALLED by God from birth, but they are awakened through encounter. Up to the point of encounter, the potential is there. The hardware is there. The gifts are there. The tools for the assignment are there. But until a prophet is sanctified to the Lord, she is desecrated by a lack of deliverance. Prophetic people have to encounter God. They have to experience God. That is what sanctifies their ministry and makes it true.

God will put His hand on the life of a prophet to introduce Himself to the prophet. This can occur before birth, sometime in childhood, or later on in life. The Lord called Samuel as a prepubescent boy. He called Ezekiel in open visions by a river. He called Jeremiah as a young child. And He called Amos in the middle of his career. God arrests and starts the gripping process on a prophetic vessel in different ways.

What does it look like to encounter God? Numbers 12 tells us God spoke to Aaron about His manner of summoning prophets. He said:

> Hear now my words: If there be a prophet among you, I the LORD will make myself known unto him in a vision, and will speak unto him in a dream.
>
> —NUMBERS 12:6

Now, you may be familiar with this verse. A lot of prophetic materials use this verse to imply dreams and visions are the primary ways God speaks to and through prophets. But that is scripturally inaccurate. In this verse God is not stating a policy for the primary, most consistent ways He deals with the prophet. That's not what it says. It says, "If there is a prophet among you, *I will make myself known to him* in a vision. I will speak to him in a dream." What's the topic? God making Himself known, not God speaking through dreams and visions. There is a difference.

When God wants to ready a prophetic vessel, His first priority is to introduce Himself.

The problem with assuming the other interpretation of this verse is that it causes everyone who has dreams and visions to assume and assert prophetic responsibility. Too often the authors of this era presume having dreams and visions qualifies a person to be a prophet. That's not always true.

Look at what Deuteronomy 13:1 tells us. There God says, "If there arise among you a prophet, or a dreamer of dreams…" Here two streams of prophetic beings are listed: prophets and dreamers of dreams. They're two separate streams, not one and the same. A prophet may dream, and a prophet may have visions. But back in Numbers 12:6 the subject matter is God's policy for making Himself known.

Let's start at the beginning. When God wants to ready a prophetic vessel, His first priority is to introduce Himself. He does this through a bizarre experience—a dream or a vision—so that the prophet will never be able to talk himself or herself out of that identity. God spends the formative years of a prophet's development making the prophet understand he or she is not normal. Prophets do not have to provoke or conjure up supernatural experiences. Those experiences find them.

Most times these experiences occur before the prophet has had the opportunity to develop language for it. You just remember growing up as a child with bizarre moments and unusual things happening to you or around you. You have adventures with God, even in the night and in your sleep.

Dreams are important from this angle. When a person is in the dream realm, God has an opportunity to communicate without interference. That is because you cannot will yourself to dream. There is no scientific explanation for why people dream. The mind does not have the capacity, of its own accord, to see the future. God visits prophets in their sleep because that is when He has their undivided attention. He begins to say things, do things, and allow experiences like this to wake up the spirit of that prophet. That is how our eyes are opened.

GOD MADE KNOWN

If we are prophets, our eyes need to be opened. I'm not talking about our natural eyes here but our spiritual perception. This is induced through our encounters with God. That's how we get to know God. There are budding prophets out there right now who are going to be powerful prophets once their eyes are opened. But the eyes don't open at will. They open upon an experience with God.

Prophets are born with the skill sets, gifts, and aptitudes needed to fulfill their calling in the spirit, but it is expressed through their souls. And the way the soul of the prophet and the spirit of the prophet are brought into alignment is through the person's experiences with God, which may be through dreams; visions; worship encounters; Bible study, which I call Word habitations; and the like.

Now, some people prophesy and do prophetic things

but have yet to really meet God. When they do meet God, that mantle will wake up. Their eyes will wake up. Their gifts will turn differently. They'll become more accurate. They'll become more specific. They will no longer prophesy from a reservoir of spiritual ability but from a history with God.

If we are prophets, our eyes need to be opened. But the eyes don't open at will. They open upon an experience with God.

This is so important. People who prophesy strictly from spiritual ability cap off at that level or that ability. But men and women who prophesy from their history with God have a much different range of prophetic scope. Eternity past, eternity present, and eternity future open up to them. They literally have access to everything God knows. That's bigger than giftedness and a person's prophetic ability!

When I talk about prophets' eyes being opened, I'm talking about their sensitivity to the unseen world—all of its events and all of its happenings. God has made Himself known to them.

Back in Numbers 12:6, the potential person God was referencing was still a prophet, even though God had not been made known to them. Again, it says, *"If there is a prophet among you…"* That reminds us, yet again, that a person is born a prophet, and he is still a prophet even if he has not met God. Thus, you can be a prophet and not know Him. Think on that.

When God makes Himself known to a prophet, the prophet's eyes pop open. They pop open so wide, they are never able to unsee what they saw.

I wonder if some of the people we have received and revered as prophets were still trying to get acquainted with the God who called them. I'm certain their abilities still worked. The gifts and the callings of God are irrevocable, after all. You're born with the ability. But you have to journey into God and into His Word and His world to know the deeper things of God. Certain things God speaks about transcend our human understanding. This is why He has to open our eyes.

When God makes Himself known to a prophet, the prophet's eyes pop open. They pop open so wide, they are never able to unsee what they saw. No matter how much the person tries to suppress it, run from it, avoid it, or postpone it, she will never be able to act as if nothing happened. The opening of the eyes is very important.

Additionally, in Jeremiah 23, during a long treatise and midsection about prophets, we read the following: "Can any hide himself in secret places that I shall not see him? saith the LORD. Do not I fill heaven and earth?" (Jer. 23:24). God sees. And God wants the human race to be aware that He sees. The prophetic ministry keeps people conscious of that reality.

That is part of who and what prophets are in the body of Christ: the eyes of the Lord. What can a blind bride do? She can't discern her bridegroom. She can't walk down the aisle on her own to present herself. Yet the Bible says, "Rejoice, for the bride has made herself ready." (See Revelation 19:7.) Readiness is not possible if you don't know what you're looking at, preparing for, or gazing toward. Sight is a powerful component, and every prophet needs to know it, consider the power of it, examine the range of it, and study what life is like without it.

The reality is that prophets are the eyes of the Lord on earth. And the Scriptures teach us these things about the eyes of the Lord:

> I will instruct you and teach you in the way which you should go; I will counsel you with My eye upon you.
>
> —Psalm 32:8, nasb

> Behold, the eye of the Lord is on those who fear Him, on those who hope for His lovingkindness.
>
> —Psalm 33:18, nasb

> For His eyes are upon the ways of a man, and He sees all his steps.
>
> —Job 34:21, nasb

> The eyes of the LORD are in every place, watching the evil and the good.
>
> —PROVERBS 15:3, NASB

> For the eyes of the LORD are toward the righteous, and His ears attend to their prayer, but the face of the LORD is against those who do evil.
>
> —1 PETER 3:12, NASB

If you were to do a diligent study of all of those verses, it would change your prophesying. If you as a prophet ministered from the position of serving as the eyes of the Lord, then saying what God sees would be enough to penetrate any soul, any heart, and any cultural barrier.

That's why I love the prophetic. It is as big as God.

PASS IT ON

When a prophet's eyes are opened, a part of his or her prophetic lifestyle is to then cause that phenomenon to happen in others. Prophets carry the ability to make people see what they have not previously seen. They have the ability, through their ministry, their prophesying, and their prayers, to change another person's optic concentration. Think about that!

The primary story related to this is found in 2 Kings 6. There the Bible says Elijah and his servant went up before another army and that the servant panicked because it looked like the Assyrian army outnumbered them. Elijah then prayed a prayer that is a classic feature of the prophet's mantle. It was not complicated. It was not complex. Elijah simply said, "Lord, open his eyes." (See verse 17.)

Instantly the man was able to perceive burning chariots. But those chariots didn't arrive when Elijah prayed. Elijah's prayer didn't put the horses or the angelic staff there. They were already there. Elijah's prayer made the servant able to see them.

Think about the implications of this. If we had more prophets with open eyes, maybe we would also have fewer people living blind in the world. The prophets would help more people know there is something more in this world, and they would live accordingly. I don't think we conceptualize why that is really important. But think about what happens when the opposite is true. When people live, decide, and act as if this realm is not attached to another, they inevitably live destructively, casually, or flirtatiously. But when people live with true awareness of God's realm, they live with a greater reverence for the deeds and the doings of their lives.

If prophets abandon their spiritual obligations, the realm we don't see becomes largely unmanaged. But God wants the eyes of His people open. In Ephesians 1 Paul prayed that "the eyes of your understanding [be] enlightened" (v. 18).

THE DEVIL'S TARGET

I believe we have limited a lot of prophetic ministry to "eyes wide shut." Many prophets are insecure and struggle to fully embrace their identity as prophets. They are afraid to allow people to know they are as strange as they are and as sensitive to the spirit world as they are. This is one way the devil keeps God's vision from being known. The devil loads a prophetic life with so much self-consciousness that the person never sees God the right way. When a prophet is self-conscious, it gets in the way of turning the prophet's consciousness toward God, thereby limiting his or her ability to speak for Him.

Many prophets don't want people to think they are strange; however, a synonym for *strange* is *supernatural*. It means to be opened up and to be aware of the fact that there is an unseen world. Prophets to the body of Christ are charged with keeping that awareness. We cannot live like this is the only world. We can't marry and teach and study and pursue and feel like there is no invisible world. Paul said the things that are unseen are eternal (2 Cor. 4:18). Prophets have the ability to deal with blindness in the body of Christ, which is why God wakes them up.

Every prophet in the world needs to be affirmed with these words: *You are not cursed.* Having open eyes and a sensitivity to the unseen world is not a curse. You may be rejected by family or by a certain group, but all prophets have to go through rejection to some extent. It's what gets the fear of man out of them. But your gift does not ruin you. It does not poison you.

The devil loads a prophetic life with so much self-consciousness that the person never sees God the right way. When a prophet is self-conscious, it gets in the way of turning the prophet's consciousness toward God, thereby limiting his or her ability to speak for Him.

One way the devil is assaulting the prophets is by discipling regular people to seek knowledge of the invisible world from ungodly sources. To learn and explore the supernatural, people find witches who have rats and jewels and cards, and they trust that those witches have more access to the future than those of us who are the servants of the living God. The occultists and white witches believe in a third eye. They believe there is an eye in the center of the forehead that allows people to have paths and portals into the invisible world to make soulless decisions. It's demonic. And yet people believe it and seek after the knowledge these occultists have.

And the church is convincing and preaching and leading as though prophecy is not necessary. How brilliant is the devil to use our own technology against us? How is it that the devil is opening eyes and the church is closing them? Is that not crazy?

Satan and the power of hell did not invent dreams.

They did not invent future-telling or forecasting. They didn't invent diverse languages to be translated and encoded. Even the gift of tongues and interpretation is a method of expedient divine communication. That's why it showed up in Acts 2—to communicate the message of the Almighty. That gift was born to communicate to the masses quickly. It was apostolic expedience, not a Charismatic toy. God knew the quickest way to communicate the same message to several nations in a matter of hours. That is our heritage. Daniel understood; he said, "There is a God in heaven who reveals secrets" (Dan. 2:28, NKJV). We need to keep our eyes open.

Jesus Christ was angry about the persecution of the prophets. Why? Because if they are the choice vessels that open up sight for all of us, it is impossible for people to see God properly without them.

You can do that—have your eyes open—and be professional and successful and a good husband or a good wife. The stigma says that a person who has the gift of sight is going to somehow be a flaky, irresponsible, or inconsistent person. In fact, the devil works immediately once a prophetic person suspects he or she has the gift. Immediately shame, condemnation, embarrassment, self-deception, and self-hatred scream, "Hide and stay away!" This is meant to convince you not to explore the power within you, the ability to see the future.

But think about what would happen if prophetic people had those very fundamental affirmations at the beginning of their ministry. We are challengers. We are working against generations of degradation. Jesus Christ was angry about the persecution of the prophets. He had a problem with people who killed prophets. Why? Because if they are the choice vessels that open up sight for all of us, it is impossible for people to see God properly without them. Therefore, the plan of salvation can be obscured. The plan of grace can be obscured.

The vocal ministries, the optic ministries, and the people who are responsible for revealing the truth about God to people have been degraded. Think about how much teaching we have to labor through to develop and be accepted by the body of Christ. The church is centuries old, yet prophets have to compete with trustees and deacons to even exist and have input into the direction of the body. I shared earlier that the church was built upon us! Ephesians 2:20 says the church is "built on the foundation of the apostles and prophets, Christ Jesus Himself being the corner stone" (NASB). The apostles and the prophets—those are the ministries and anointings responsible for upholding Jesus Christ. These two mantles were present at the beginning of the church, and the church has no future without them.

We need eyes wide open. We need prophets who say, "Yes, I see the invisible. My emotions are fine. I'm not going to lose my mind or end up in a crazy house." But when prophetic people are taught to despise their gift, they do go crazy. Imagine how the devil works overtime to drive prophets crazy. He hates prophets. He hates everybody, really. But do you know who he hates the most? People who have the capacity to see him. Satan's worst fights are with the people who see him.

If you don't believe me, look at what women have been going through since the garden. Women have been persecuted, abused, and degraded throughout history. Can you believe that in some nations women still don't have rights? In some places they can't drive or show their face. Satan has been aggressively fighting the female species since the Garden of Eden. Why? Because Eve saw him.

Similarly, prophets see him. Even more importantly, prophets see God and what God sees. They herald, "Turn on the lights. That's not God. That's deception." And so Satan has to kill them off.

It is our ministry to expose, to turn the light on, to see, and to be clear. Wherever the lights are on, the works of hell are weakened.

The strength of Satan's entire kingdom is darkness. But God is light. In Him there is no darkness at all (1 John 1:5). Revelation 22:5 says that at the end of time, there will be no need for the sun, because the Lord will give us light. Jesus is legitimately—not figuratively or religiously—the light of the world (John 8:12). He meant that. And without Jesus Christ's sovereignty over the world we have no light. He is the light of the world.

It is our ministry to expose, to turn the light on, to see, and to be clear. Wherever the lights are on, the works of hell are weakened. We ought to cry out, "Turn on the lights in me!" Think about what the Scriptures say. When the eyes are clear, the whole body is full of light (Matt. 6:22). So eyes and light are congruent.

This is why the devil employs a myriad of ways to kill the ministry of the prophets. He's using preachers to do it. He used the early church fathers and Roman Catholics to do it. He's using everything in the world to do it. He seeks to make prophets implode, to make them hate their sensitivity and awareness.

I encourage prophets to study the biblical prophets for this reason. Think about how those prophets had their own demented moments, times when they despised the day of their birth or their sight. "Cursed be the day I was born," Jeremiah said (Jer. 20:14, NIV). Habakkuk asked, "Why do you make me see?" (Hab. 1:3, ESV). They went deep into the realm of despair because of their inability to handle their gift to perceive and to know.

A quote I say all the time is, "Many are the woes

of the one gifted with prophetic sight." A life of prophetic sight is a life of great pain, not because it causes pain to come upon you but because seeing things as they are can be painful. Nevertheless, someone has to do it. The church has no future if she has no eyes.

CHAPTER 6

Face-to-Face Encounters

FOLLOWING THE LAST chapter's focus on encountering God so that our eyes are opened, let's talk about the power of encounters with God. It is my belief that you can always find out or trace the ministry of a prophet based on how he met God. The way a prophet meets God will reveal a lot about what he will eventually be called by God to do. I call it a "prophetic introduction." It's how God confronts the life of someone who is going to carry His word.

Take the prophet Ezekiel, for instance. When Ezekiel was sitting by the River Chebar, he had visions of God, "and the hand of the LORD was there upon him" (Ezek. 1:3). Ezekiel saw a whirlwind coming out of the north and a great cloud with fire engulfing itself. He saw brightness all around the cloud and radiating out of its midst like the color of amber (Ezek. 1:4). Through those visions, Ezekiel saw the splendor and glory of God, which was important because during his ministry he would deliver hard words to a people the Bible called stiff-necked.

I believe God started Ezekiel off in the prophetic by showing him beautiful things because God ultimately would give him visions of hard things. And he needed to remember that the One who called him is good and even the hard things from God are good. Also, those hard words had to come from a good place in Ezekiel's heart, not a place of bitterness or fear. So God showed him the good first and out of that revelation of God, Ezekiel gained the bravery to deliver the hard words to the nation.

When God called the prophet Jeremiah, He reached out and touched Jeremiah's mouth and said, "I have put my words in thy mouth" (Jer. 1:9). In his ministry Jeremiah preached throughout Israel, declaring the word of the Lord, and later God instructed him to write down the early prophetic words He had given him.

Elisha was called to be a prophet when Elijah threw his mantle over him (1 Kings 19:19–21). Elisha followed Elijah, learning from and serving him. We don't know how Elisha may have encountered God or how God may have revealed Himself to Elisha while he was being mentored by Elijah. When Elijah was taken up to heaven, God gave Elisha a double portion of the anointing he had been observing as he walked with Elijah.

God reveals Himself to a prophet before He begins to speak to that prophet, and the way He introduces Himself is often indicative of how God will use that prophet. The beautiful thing is that as a prophetic person continues her relationship with God, God continues to reveal, or reintroduce, Himself to the prophet. A prophetic vessel is going to see God in a number of different ways over her lifetime. As God reveals Himself more and more to that prophetic person, her prophetic ability will increase. Why? Because the more we see God, the more we understand things through His lens. Our capacity grows.

There is power in talking to a man or woman who sees God's face all the time. The inroad to error in the prophetic movement was that we didn't make it encounter-based or experiential. Instead, we made it about prophetic ability alone. But getting acquainted with the personality of God—the nature of God and His being—deepens the power within a prophet. You speak best for people you know well.

A SECURE FRIENDSHIP

If a prophet is a friend of God, then God has to do a lot to perfect His friendship with that prophet. That's what He did with Moses. That's what He did with Ezekiel. He worked on their friendship. The Book of Psalms tells us that "the secret of the LORD is with them that fear him" (Ps. 25:14). That is friendship with God.

There are a lot of people God does not trust or confide in because they are not good friends to Him. When a man or woman shows up with a desire to befriend God, that person opens his or her life up for a lifestyle of encounters.

Now, encounters with God, to a prophetic person, are not Him coming to entertain you. A God encounter is not something you receive for the sake of showing off. He gets glory from it, but ultimately He is trying to reveal Himself to you and to others.

God is so big that one person does not have enough time in his or her lifetime to fully see the facets of who and how He is. This is why He reveals Himself in so many ways in the Scriptures. It all rings true. He is everything He was ever revealed to be in the Scriptures—and more.

So, the possibilities you have to experience Him are very broad. He can look like a wheel within a wheel, as described in Ezekiel 1. He can show Himself through a bush that is burning but not consumed. He can be seen in a vision of an ox or an eagle. He can speak to you as the incarnate Son of God. And it is all Him.

These encounters happen partly so a prophetic person becomes secure and doesn't leave his calling. An encounter is God's preventative measure to keep a prophet from going rogue. I speak from experience here. God allowed encounters in my life and in the lives of a lot of the prophetic people I've tried to raise up, and those encounters have demonstrated to me the truth that if you have seen Him and experienced Him, it is virtually impossible to act as if He does not exist.

God experiences and God encounters, when they happen, are going to be revelatory. God will appear. He will show you things. He will open up His world to yours to share things with you.

If you have seen Him and experienced Him, it is virtually impossible to act as if He does not exist.

But there will also be times when He allows you to experience Him devotionally in worship to make sure there is enough of Him in your knowledge base and in your experience that you never think to leave Him. God is highly concerned that people who carry His word do not leave Him. So encounters are God's retention plan. They are how God keeps a prophet near. They are how He opens prophets up to heavenly experiences. He makes sure their hearts are wired in Him.

DRAWN TO DRAW OTHERS

God does not want to be known just through His voice. He wants to be experienced. He wants to be explored. If we restrict the prophetic to what He has to say alone, then we limit our other ability, which is to bring people into what the Bible calls fellowship with the Son of God, to "know Him and the power of His resurrection" (Phil. 3:10, NKJV). That is coming into the undeniable reality that the God of the whole earth is alive and actively pursuing every heart that is not in His hand.

Our devotion is our pursuit of God, but an encounter happens because of His pursuit of us—and it is through that "life arrest" that He becomes more real.

God is progressively pursuing the heart of every human being on the planet, even when they don't want Him. He is a pursuing God. Nobody knows that like a prophet who has encountered Him. A prophet cannot manufacture an encounter. He can't just go to sleep or wake up in the morning and say, "Hey, today I think I want to be visited." Visitation is a manifestation of God's pursuit. He initiates it.

Our devotion is our pursuit of God, but an encounter happens because of His pursuit of us—and it is through that "life arrest" that He becomes more real and more real and more real.

The prophet's ministry is how the human heart of every species knows that God is real. He proves Himself through the prophetic. Now, that is a simple statement, but it's loaded. *He proves Himself through the prophetic.* There are people who don't even realize that God has something to prove, but He does. The Bible says God has been proving Himself and will continue to show Himself strong throughout the ages (2 Chron. 16:9).

How does God do that? By inviting a person to experience Him. Think about how powerful it is to be the type of person who can open up another person not just to hear God but to make the person aware that God knows them. Even witches can get people's secret information. It's deeper than that for us. Our secret information leads to a greater revelation.

See, one of the problems with witchcraft is that a soothsayer, predictor, or diviner will never tell you that what they reveal comes from one being. Witches and occultists who hack into supernatural information give people information without attributing it to one source. It comes from the moon; it comes from the universe; it comes from the earth. Sometimes it comes from the dead. It can come from ghosts and from roaming spirits. So their "revelation" does not reveal one person. It just reveals that they somehow have invisible information about people's lives.

But that is what makes the prophet's role so powerful. Our information leads to the revelation of a Person: Jesus Christ. Whenever the prophetic is detached from revealing Jesus Christ, it has gone perverse.

The fruit of matured revelation is relationship. Every

deity, every god, has its representative. The ultimate objective of all we do and all we say and all we push is to reveal the Son of Man as He is—not just how we see Him, but as He is. That is the intrinsic ministry and nature of the prophet. God expresses Himself by using a human vessel or a human conduit so He can be understood and heard. But that vessel has to be tempered enough to be sensitive to knowing what God sounds like, and God equips a prophetic person to do that by revealing Himself. When revelation does not flow from or for relationship, connecting people back to God, it cannot produce righteousness. I believe that God's greatest desire is to be experienced—not to just be heard, or even to be thought of or regarded, but to be experienced.

Think about how few people would backslide if they experienced the God that they are trying to live for. It is a simple principle, but a lot of people never really get to experience the God they believe in. They *believe* in Him, but a lot of them backslide. The heart was created to explore the Almighty. It's a heart thing. This is what Paul was writing about when he talked about how deep, how far, and how wide (Eph. 3:18). Those are ranges of God's personhood that can be explored and experienced, although no one alive would have enough time to do so.

The prophetic is powerful because the prophet can push people further and further into experiencing

God. Through pain, we can do it. We can do it when people are backsliding. I love the fact that the prophetic can end the wavering and wandering of the heart. When a life is vacillating to and fro between possibilities, options, and choices, the prophetic can settle the issue.

Whenever the prophetic is detached from revealing Jesus Christ, it has gone perverse.

Elijah said, "How long will you falter between two opinions?" (1 Kings 18:21, NKJV). Every human being has the potential to be stunted, sometimes for years, between two opinions of who they're going to be, what they're going to do, how they're going to move, how they're going to set up their family, or how they're going to set up their career. The prophetic can end the whole discussion and push people into a life of experiencing God and experiencing Jesus.

There is power when people experience their God, when they see Him and know Him and His character. There are times, if you study God encounters in the Bible, where God's world ran into a human's world and the person saw Him or had a vision and suddenly knew things but didn't know how.

Consider Paul's Damascus encounter, for example. He didn't believe in Jesus and was a murderer of Jews. However, as soon as he saw that light shone from heaven, he fell on his face, and the first thing that came out of his mouth was, "Lord, Lord." The first thing out of the man's mouth was the designation of a surrendered life. He called Him "Lord." An encounter will do that to you. It has the power to suddenly erase all of a person's suspicions toward God and cause that individual to see Him as He is.

There is power when people experience their God, when they see Him and know Him and His character.

If you see who God is, then you'll do what He wants. You'll understand what He is doing. God can get our hearts to cooperate as we experience Him. When I talk about face-to-face encounters, I mean that in a symbolic sense. I'm not talking about a person having to literally see the face of God. I'm just talking about exploring parts of Him. All prophets have had marked moments when they saw Him. You can tear up thinking about it.

Some of your encounters with God become life markers, pivotal points of when things are about to begin or sometimes even when things end. There are prophetic people who have encounters with God as a point of deliverance. That encounter with God will pull them out of something, and that's how they are encouraged and motivated to stay out.

Encounters are a very profound resource for the

backslidden. When we can't reach them through witnessing or invitation or preaching, they can be arrested in an encounter where they are undeniably seeing God, and that has a powerful impact on the heart. Think about it. Someone says, "I don't think God is real," and then He becomes real as something that science cannot explain occurs.

Now, when a prophet says yes to God, a part of what she is signing up for is a life of back-to-back experiences with God. Those experiences will be different. But they will all achieve the same thing, which is to keep the prophet in relationship and to anoint her to cause relationship. As I prophesy, I have the powerful responsibility of bringing people either into relationship or into a deeper relationship with Jesus Christ.

Every opportunity to prophesy can bring people out of an estranged status with God. If a life has been estranged from God, or if there is some form of discord between a person and God, the prophetic can close the gap and heal communication. It literally is divine counsel.

If God has unfinished business or something to work out in a person's life, prophets become counselors. They can present God's will and purpose and heart to a person with the ultimate objective of reconciling the individual with Him. This is always God's heart.

There has to be in our revelation a redemptive component where we can find God in everything and help people to find God in everything. This is especially vital if you have not explored the character of God and if God is not consistently welcome into your world.

It would seem the easiest way for this to happen is through prayer. I think a lot of people have God encounters in prayer because it's the time when they are most focused and when they have "set [their] heart" (Job 11:13, MSG) to seek Him. I also think nighttime is an easier time for some people because their logical mind is usually relaxed. When you're about to go to sleep or are asleep, you're not really thinking, so God can interrupt all that and have your complete attention to reveal whatever He is about to show you. This is all a part of experiencing God face to face. It's what we've already seen in Numbers 12:6 about God making Himself known to prophets in dreams and visions.

Since the beginning of all prophetic service is getting to know Him, it's dangerous to jump into prophecy before you know God well. You run the risk of misrepresenting Him. A lot of prophetic development is about getting to know Him a little better. As you grow closer to God, you start to decipher His tone, His demeanor, His attitude, His passions, and His opinions in order to become an adequate representation.

When I was in that Numbers 12:6 phase, I would have repetitive dreams that wouldn't change. I would have the same dream with no variation. Sometimes these dreams would come once a week. Other times they would come once a month. It got so bad that I would realize I was in the dream and know exactly how it was going to play out. Other dreamers will understand that feeling. I didn't realize at the time that repetition is a tool of God. There are certain truths that God wants branded on a life. Repetitive dreams, especially if they're about you, are either God's destiny for you or Satan's disaster for you. They are something to live for or something to look out for, because God is making sure this counsel is grafted in your soul.

If you jump into prophecy before you know God well, you run the risk of misrepresenting Him.

Again, dreams are one of the ways that God comes face to face with us. The human brain and soul, however complex and wonderful, do not have the ability to know the future. The basis of everything you know is history. You know how to read because you were taught historically. You understand what a boy and a girl are because you were taught historically. But you cannot know the future except by the mind of God. You have not been there. So, think about how real it is for the future to come to you by way of a dream—for what happened in the dream to be lived out as you saw it. This is God coming face to face.

BEWARE THE
MANIPULATIVE POWER

The devil will work very hard to separate a prophet from God, because then he can use those abilities to amplify the agenda of another. Even prophetic people who are not saved have the power of a spokesperson. They are going to find themselves defending people, fighting for people, or being the friend that people rely on. Every prophetic life has some degree of advocacy. Prophets are the ones everybody looks to before they make their final decisions.

Somehow, before a prophet knows who he or she is, the pressure of being the one who determines what's next is always on the prophet. They determine what is cool or what's the trend. Everybody wants to be like the prophet because the prophetic life has provisions that allow for things to open up.

The devil will work very hard to separate a prophet from God, because then he can use those abilities to amplify the agenda of another.

It is important for you to have encounters to clean all of those resources up. You have to clean them up because they can become powerfully manipulative things if you don't. Always remember there is a world bigger than ours out there. If you ever lose sight of that, you're going to make your calling just about telling people stuff, and the prophetic is not just about people telling people what to do. It's about inviting people into a relationship with revelation—where it comes from, where it exists, and why it exists.

THE POWER OF PROPHECY

In the Song of Solomon the Bible talks about how God has set eternity in our hearts. If eternity is in your heart and in the heart of every human being, we can talk to the eternity that is in every heart and give people the courage to live out what God planned for them eternally. That is the power of prophecy, and that is the power of prophesying as a person who has met the God he is speaking for. That is so important.

There are so many options for spirituality and people's approach to it. Some people have a cultural spirituality, where they consider themselves spiritual people. They don't have a person or being at the top of their spirituality; they are just kind of open to spiritual things.

There is another type of person that is a humanist or spiritist. These people believe that to be human is to be divine; however, it's the human nature of a person that makes up the whole idea that a human is god.

Then you've got the extreme version of this, where people legitimately still believe in UFOs and aliens and all that stuff. I mean, there are whole communities of people who believe those things exist. That is the human heart's way of trying to search for Jesus. And on their way to trying to find Him, they bump into spirits masquerading as aliens.

Every heart is on a journey to try to find the one in whom they believe or the one who loves them. That sets a life on pursuit. The sad reality is that a lot of people live and die right there looking for something—they just don't know what it is. That search—that thirst, that hunger—is where addiction, bondage, and more are born in a person, as people run into things that end up filling and occupying that space.

When they meet a face-to-face messenger, that messenger can offer an explanation for that life-and-heart search. It takes that kind of encounter. Think about the most powerful prophetic word you have ever received. No doubt a couple of things come to your mind. The first is where you were as a person at that time, what you did or did not believe about God, what you thought was about to happen in your life, and how that prophetic word addressed you where you were.

Every prophetic word that I remember—and there are some I remember word for word—I remember in detail. I remember where I was in life, where my heart was, the decision I was trying to make about what direction I would follow, and how the prophet could not in his flesh have known to say exactly what needed to be said in order to anchor me in my relationship with God.

The ability to do that has to come from somebody who has seen God and knows Him, someone who is able to relate to and speak to the human experience specifically, directly, and easily. That is our job. As prophets that is what we're supposed to be doing: facilitating and furthering relationship between heaven and earth.

Think about how a relationship is enriched in any context through the quality of communication. A marriage does not get better without the two people growing in their ability to communicate. Parenting does not get better if we don't learn to adapt our communication. Yet we are calling revival to a mute church.

As prophets we're supposed to be facilitating and furthering relationship between heaven and earth.

The prophetic is the way God has chosen to speak. He has something to say. So, the whole of what we do is a different approach to reaching people through relationship. It is so powerful.

We see this was the case in the garden. When Adam and Eve got lost, God's voice came to get them. It is about relationship. And if you ask God to know Him, He will respond in every way you are willing to receive. He will introduce Himself, and it will change you. If you ever really have an encounter with God, it changes you. It changes parts of you. Parts of you will die. Parts of you will come alive.

We see this in Exodus 3 when Moses encountered God in the burning bush. God dealt with Moses' fear of man through that burning bush. Moses was more scared of what he saw in that burning bush than what he knew Pharaoh could do. He was acquainted with Pharaoh. Pharaoh had raised him. That is why he asked, "Who shall I say sent me?" A greater authority came from the bush than what he had learned was in Pharaoh.

Moses was so impacted by whatever he saw in that burning bush that it weighed more than his consistent assignment to go back and forth. He would never have gone back to Egypt had he been arrested by the fear of man and what Pharaoh could have done to him. He would never have gone back had he been handicapped by his stuttering and inability. What he saw in that bush was forever sealed in his heart.

If you ask God to know Him, He will respond in every way you are willing to receive.

But have you ever thought about why a rebellious or wandering prophet gets such severe consequences? It is because this prophet, more than any other human being, has seen the reality of God. God cannot allow him to experience the same consequences as a normal human being, because he has known God in an entirely different way and carried His word. God has shown him more of Himself than He has the average person.

For example, a big fish swallowing Jonah was pretty extreme. Why were consequences of that magnitude necessary? Because of the face-to-face law—once you have seen Him, you cannot ever unsee Him. You could try to convince yourself for the rest of your life that you have not seen Him, but to know Him and to make Him known is the whole of prophetic service. It's always bad when we make the prophetic more about impressing people with ministry magic than prophesying to create relationship and facilitate discussion between heaven and earth.

COMMUNICATION IS GOD'S PRIORITY

There is so much God wants to talk about. Many discussions need to be had. Many truths need to be said. Many cycles need to end. Think about what is achieved through communication. You express yourself. You explain yourself. You communicate your desires. You communicate your experiences. Very few people understand life through the lens of God because we don't have a lot of access to His communication channels. Think about it. Prophets exist because God wants to communicate. Yet there are hearts with no clue that communication is at the top of His priorities. Those of us who are communication agents and entities need to do our best to live up to that awesome task, because at the top of God's priority list is to communicate with the human race.

Open your heart to imagine what that could solve. Every disease on planet Earth—and I'm talking about moral, national, and more—could be settled by consistent communication from the Lord. Hell is afraid of a consistent stream of information coming out of heaven. God has more ways to communicate than you have to hear. Dreams and visions and strange events, including trances and translations—these are different revelatory resources and different streams that God chooses to communicate through. Encounters with Him can open up events like these.

THE POWER OF CLOSENESS

In some God encounters you will feel things on your body. God has ways to open up every natural sense you have, including all of your five senses. Personally speaking, my favorite prophet is Samuel, but my favorite apostle is John the Revelator. In the encounters that he described in the Book of Revelation, he sometimes said he saw lights. Other times he said, "I heard a loud trumpet." He also said, "A person came up and said unto me." Every part of John's humanity was arrested by those encounters. There was no room for him to talk himself out of those experiences, and this led to the revelation of Jesus Christ.

As I've stated several ways in this chapter, revelation should initiate and cultivate relationship. This is imperative for those who believe God is distant and careless.

When done erroneously, the prophetic can come off really cold. Imagine living a dismal life and hearing from someone who claims to be a messenger of God. They have good words but no emotion or passion toward you. This often occurs with messengers who are distant from the person they're speaking for. Closeness is our power. We have to know God so well that we can persuade someone in a two-minute prophecy how close He wants to be to them and how involved He wants to be in that person's future.

Every disease on planet Earth—moral, national, and more—could be settled by consistent communication from the Lord.

Jesus said, "I am with you always, even unto the end of the world" (Matt. 28:20). What does that mean to us? In a way, it should be interpreted as the ministry of closeness. It's so important that a prophet know their God. Think about what can be achieved in a life lived close to God. What can be conquered and resolved? What can be produced?

God desires closeness. I don't think human beings

can even imagine the degree of closeness God wants to have with us. When He finally finds a man or woman like this, He takes him or her. Enoch was, and was not, and he walked with God (Gen. 5:24); he prophesied about the judgment of God, the vindication of God, and the rescue of God. Or consider Moses and his face-to-face relationship to God. God didn't even allow people to know where Moses' body was buried (Deut. 34:6). What about Elijah and the flaming horse that carried him up into the sky (2 Kings 2:11)? What does this say about these people and how God felt about their availability?

Everything God wants for human existence must be born through closeness.

The taking of Elijah was a very public display. It could have been a private matter. What if God allowed it to happen in order to provoke those watching to godly jealousy? Could that have incited hunger and thirst in hundreds of prophets, causing them to say, "Oh, I want that. I want to know Him in that way"? Very few men live up to that, but that is God's objective. He's saying, "Come closer. We could do so much more in closeness than we can at a distance."

You can't do destiny from a distance. You can't be delivered at a distance. You can't even decide well at a distance. Everything God wants for human existence must be born through closeness. Prophecy is the proximity ministry. When a person who doesn't know you can tell you who you are, where you've been, and where you're going, the natural response is to come close.

We reach the secrets of the heart (1 Cor. 14:24–25) because those hidden things are what keep people at a distance. When a prophetic person can expose and confront the secrets of the heart, it's like God is reeling the person in on a bait line.

"Come close" is God's word to this culture. The world is judging, assessing, critiquing, and analyzing Him through the lens of everything but His Word. But God is out to accurately prove Himself; thus, He chooses a face-to-face life and says through it, "I can show you better than I can tell you."

Speaking of showing versus telling, a lot of people's hostility or resistance toward God lies in their distant approach to the Bible. If we approach the Word like a document, we approach it at a distance. And if we approach it at a distance, it can't have any real weight or relevance to our decisions today. Certainly we can retrieve some principles for successful living, but God wants so much more than for us to live successful lives.

Revelation is a by-product of closeness. If you know the author of a document, what he wrote makes more sense to you. So when you get close to God, you start to approach the Scriptures a lot differently. You see more meat in the phrases. If you get close enough, the punctuation will talk to you. Everything—even the pauses—will give you insight when you are close to God.

God wants His Son manifest, and the way He does that is by calling people into closeness. The prophetic is so much more than "I saw this creature" or "I had this vision and heard this saying." Those are all attempts to bring you close so that you can become more deeply persuaded and rooted, not just in your purpose, but in His personhood. Once that occurs, you can adequately portray Him to the world and others can be brought near to Him.

When you get close to God, you start to approach the Scriptures a lot differently. You see more meat in the phrases. If you get close enough, the punctuation will talk to you. Everything— even the pauses—will give you insight.

Every generation must be reintroduced to God, and the people who do that best are the ones who see and know Him. You should never speak for and introduce a God you're still struggling to believe in. The prophetic works best in closeness.

May we never become familiar with what this calling can make possible for a distant life and secretive heart. May we never get complacent with the beautiful call to a life of fellowship and revelation.

CHAPTER 7

Diverse Expressions

ONE OF THE best known scriptures about the spiritual gifts is found in 1 Corinthians 12. Paul writes:

> Now there are diversities of gifts, but the same Spirit. And there are differences of administrations, but the same Lord. And there are diversities of operations, but it is the same God which worketh all in all.
>
> —1 CORINTHIANS 12:4–6

Paul uses three words here: *gifts*, *administrations*, and *operations*. And the important thing to know is that each of the gifts can have different administrations and different operations. Two people can have the same gift, but they can operate differently in each person. For example, if a person has the gifting of the word of wisdom, she can prophesy accurately concerning the future or dream a word of wisdom. It's the same gift but utilized differently. Or think of dreaming of the future. That is a manifestation of the gift of the word of wisdom, but the gift of the word of knowledge can work in the same way. If a fact that can be proven is revealed to you in a dream, that is a manifestation of the word of knowledge.

The point here is that there is a broad range of gifts and how they manifest and how they operate—which is why there is never any room for comparison.

ALL THE MANY FACETS

We all have similar gift sets that operate differently. Even in the Bible we see a broad range of prophetic administrations and expressions. And it would be weird to see some of those biblical expressions at work in our current world. Accordingly, God has unlimited ways of declaring and demonstrating His word.

In this chapter we will look at the various expressions that can flow through those called to the prophetic.

Drama

First of all, the prophetic typifies heaven's drama. Prophetic people have a dramatic capability. Sometimes the word of the Lord is manifested most profoundly in a dramatic presentation, depending upon its details. For example, remember when Agabus went to give Paul the word of the Lord? (See Acts 21:10–11.) Instead of saying, "God said you're going to go to jail," Agabus walked up to the apostle, took his belt, and bound his hands and feet to give the message that was given to him. Now, Agabus wasn't a cop, so what was he doing? He was demonstrating the word of the Lord. Some things are better seen than heard.

There is a broad range of gifts and how they manifest and how they operate—which is why there is never any room for comparison.

Another degree of prophesying comes through acting and dramatization of the word of the Lord. Ezekiel would build things, lay on his side, and eat scrolls. He portrayed God's heart through very unusual acts.

But the word of the Lord is so powerful, it can captivate in more than one way. Part of what God uses the word to do is to captivate and to capture, and yet we usually limit prophetic expression to the vocal aspects. However, the word of the Lord can be conveyed in a lot of different ways.

Singing

Singing is another way the prophet can express the word of the Lord. Lots of biblical prophets wrote songs. Prophets in the Books of Chronicles were responsible for staffing David's temple, and we notice that most of these singing prophets were considered seers. And probably because of the environmental component, they changed things with song.

Counsel

Another common way to deliver the word of the Lord is through prophetic counsel. This is the same as prophesying but is done conversationally. A classic example is how Nathan delivered the word of the Lord to David. (See 2 Samuel 12:1–15.) Another example less commonly considered is Moses with Pharaoh. When Moses told Pharaoh, "Let my people go," that was a prophetic conversation. Every time Moses went to Pharaoh, he said what God told him to say. Those were prophetic words.

Prophetic intercessors are able to move things in the spirit, to cause situations to shift and atmospheres to change, because they pray the heart and mind of God, and the Lord backs what they say to bring forth His plans and purposes.

Councils

A somewhat unusual prophetic expression that I believe we're going to see more of is the prophetic council. This is when people come to tables and gatherings of prophets to search for prophetic consensus. In the Bible kings would often summon all of the prophets of the land. The group that met Saul on Mount Gilboa before his encounter with the prophet

Samuel is an example of a prophetic council. (See 1 Samuel 28:4–6.) Group prophesying is a powerful form of prophetic expression. I believe we should have more formalized versions of these around events like presidential elections.

Intercession

Prophetic intercession is a form of prophetic administration and one of the ways prophecy works. All true prophets are intercessors, but not all intercessors are prophets. Because intercessors spend so much time in prayer, they will certainly perceive things in the spirit. But God will share His secrets with prophetic intercessors so they can pray His will into situations and cause His will to manifest in the physical world. Prophetic intercessors are able to move things in the spirit, to cause situations to shift and atmospheres to change, because they pray the heart and mind of God, and the Lord backs what they say to bring forth His plans and purposes.

Interpretation of dreams

Another administration of prophecy—and a powerful one—is the interpretation of dreams. It's also a very powerful prophetic expression. I believe it is a necessity if we are going to reach agnostics, as interpreting dreams has the power to pull people out of indifference. Look at what happened when Daniel used this approach. He told Nebuchadnezzar his dream and its interpretation, and that resulted in the king's acknowledgment of Daniel's God. (See Daniel 2.)

Very seldom do we see people whose ministry involves the interpretation of dreams. Think about how useful that could be and how far the prophetic could reach if we didn't rely only on traditional prophesying but incorporated approaches like this one—especially because dreams are one way God troubles people He wants to deal with who won't hear Him otherwise. However, such an experience should always be done in tandem with a prophetic anointing, as these kinds of dreams must be interpreted.

Dream interpretation is how we came to understand the revelation of God as the revealer of secrets. The prophetic has the capacity to trace what happens in people's sleep activity. We cannot physically go into a person's sleep life, but there is a way for it to be revealed.

Imagine how many people, evangelistically speaking, would be deeply moved with this demonstration, particularly in cases of nightmares or repetitive dreams. Imagine the power of being able to confidently say, "You've been having a repetitive dream since you were this age. Here's what it is, and this is what it means." That is a prophetic word and a very powerful and rare manifestation. We need to press into that.

Miracles

Miraculous prophecies are another expression of the prophetic gift. Again, consider Elisha and Naaman. (See 2 Kings 5:1–14.) When Naaman had leprosy, what did Elisha do? He prophesied what Naaman was to do—wash in the Jordan River seven times—and when Naaman did so, he was healed. That is a signs and wonders prophecy. These are powerful prophecies that open miracles.

Another example is Elijah and the widow's oil. (See 1 Kings 17:8–16.) Elijah told the widow that the oil would not be extinguished until there was rain on the earth, and it was so. That, again, is prophecy that translated God's miraculous reserves into the earth. It is an example of someone prophesying things by power, and that thing happening by power.

Lifestyle

Some prophets are called to lifestyle prophecy, where God has a prophet live out a message they will later prophesy. Hosea is one example of this. God told Hosea, "Marry this whore and say to the people, 'You have been unfaithful unto me.'" (See Hosea 1:2.) The whole point was to live out the word of the Lord. Then he prophesied with a greater acquaintance with God's perspective.

Have you ever thought about the power of living out a prophecy? I think that happens in a lot of prophets. They can live out a word and then call the body of

Christ into what happened. Hosea experienced first-hand God's feelings in response to Israel's unfaithfulness. God wanted to reach for agony in Hosea, so He made Hosea live out His word.

Burden-bearing

Another prophetic administration is burden-bearing. This is common in prophetic counselors and prophetic intercessors. Many of the prophets would speak of the burden of the Lord or say, "The hand of the Lord came upon me." What does that mean? It's when the weight of a prophetic word affects your entire mood, your entire day, and your entire demeanor. That's burden-bearing.

Burden-bearing, in itself, is a ministry. It's useful in intercession. When you feel burdened about something, you pray a lot differently than when you're just thinking about it. There are times when prophets start to feel things in their emotional self. A mature prophet will be able to translate those feelings into the word of the Lord. If a prophet's ministry is prayer, he or she wants to be hypersensitive to the burden-bearing reality. That's what intercession is—going to prayer in the burden of the Lord. A prophetic intercessor will pray himself or prophesy herself until the burdens lifts.

When the weight of a prophetic word affects your entire mood, your entire day, and your entire demeanor, that's burden-bearing.

Burdens are powerful, and real prophets know that. When something really grips you, it almost annoys you until you've found what to do to act. You just cannot shake it. Burdens kept the biblical prophets up very late and woke them up very early. They are manifestations of one of God's ways to communicate the word of the Lord.

Decrees

Prophetic decrees are another expression of the prophetic ministry. These are prophetic declarations. While some prophetic words are communicated in conversation, in council, in song, or in prayer, other times a prophetic word can be declared.

All prophetic words are uttered, but not all of them are uttered in declarative form. Sometimes, for example, through the Old Testament prophets, God asked rhetorical questions. He would also warn, which is another type of prophetic administration. But when God would declare things over people through prophets, He would speak of a reality yet to come. That is what a declaration is. The traditional term for it is *forth-telling*, but I want to call it "force-telling." These are things you declare into existence. "Declaring the end," Isaiah says, "from the beginning" (Isa. 46:10). Declaring the end from before the beginning is like force-telling, or forth-telling.

Dancing

Another very powerful prophetic administration, believe it or not, is dancing. I believe the word of the Lord can be danced out. Messages can be interpreted by dance, as the prophet Miriam showed us. She incited a revelatory revolution as a prophetess who danced and sang the word of the Lord. (See Exodus 15:20–21.) That had to be one well-choreographed dance, because what she sang about was not necessarily celebratory! It was a war song, so it was likely very aggressive. And when she began to dance, the women she led responded. That is a powerful prophetic administration. Maybe we need to see more dancing prophets.

---

*Dancing is a powerful way to prophesy.
It's more than skill and rhythm. It's
dancing with and in revelation*

But speaking of dancing, I've seen demons jump out of people who were dancing around. I don't have a full explanation for this, but I know it's one of the ways the word of the Lord manifests. God had to use it. There is a message in movement. It expresses and conveys.

If you think about the power of dance and dance technology, it is native to every race on the planet. Everyone responds to melody, responds to rhythm, and responds to music. It would be fitting that dance has a revelatory component. What does the song and the sound make you feel, make you see, and make you concentrate on? It is a powerful way to prophesy. It's more than skill and rhythm. It's dancing with and in revelation—and it can almost make you want to dance.

Now, in some places, you find dancers doing cheesy, repetitive movements. But then there are those who are full of the emotion of God and nearly come out of their bodies when they dance. This demonstration goes into some very profound things. It would do wonders to a person in need of deliverance.

Going back to the story of Miriam and Moses, their song and dance happened after the people had been freed from slavery, having walked through the Red Sea on dry land. Now, captives don't usually have the right to dance or the freedom to dance. Slaves find it difficult to arouse that kind of joy in an oppressed life. Maybe the reason Miriam danced was for prophetic cooperation. It was her way of communicating to the people, "You are free. You are no longer slaves."

Artistry

Next there is prophetic artistry. If you believe in prophetic visions, you should believe in prophetic art. Art captures imagery from the invisible world. If people can have visions and see pictures of things that communicate, it is only fitting that people be able to translate those images into legitimate colors, pictures, and hues that stand as monuments.

Naming

A lot of people in the Bible would name their kids prophetically. There are a lot of people today who name their children prophetically. I believe that a person's name is one of the most powerful prophetic words he or she will ever have. Think about how many people in the Bible received their name by revelation.

Instrumentation

Instrumentation is another type of prophetic act. The Bible says that men prophesied upon harps. The way music is played can be a prophetic expression or a prophetic message or word. Saul called for David to play so that deliverance could happen. (See 1 Samuel 16:23.)

Environments

God can speak to a person anywhere, but there were times when He led prophets to certain places before He spoke to them. For instance, He puts prophets in the environment of that word or the reality of that revelation so they will not take it for granted and will fully conceptualize what God is saying. One example of this is a trance, where the word of God will arrest a person for an amount of time to communicate something to him or her in a vision.

Actions

There are also prophetic acts or actions. When the mantle fell on Elisha, that was a word, a prophetic act. It did something to Elisha. It didn't make Elisha *become* Elisha. He was always Elisha. But when the mantle fell, it was an announcement of what was next.

The Bible is full of such prophetic acts, where people did things in response to or in accordance with the word of the Lord. Elisha lying on top of a dead body—that was a prophetic act that spoke the word of the Lord. (See 2 Kings 4:32–37.) We see it as an act, but he could have done it vocally. The same is true about when Jesus stood up for the woman caught in the act of adultery. (See John 8:3–11.) He got down and wrote it in the sand. He acted out a word. He did something that communicated God's heart. That was a prophetic act.

When the mantle fell on Elisha, that was a prophetic act. It didn't make Elisha become Elisha. It was an announcement of what was next.

Here's another one. Remember when the king sought out Elisha for help? Elisha told him, "Open the window and shoot out the arrow, saying, 'This is the arrow of the Lord's deliverance.'" (See 2 Kings 13:14–19.) He could have prophesied it, but he had the king open the east window and pull out an arrow.

Prophetic acts were heavy in the ministries of Elijah and Elisha. They would do things in response to the word of the Lord. One of my favorite prophetic acts from Elijah was his altar-building. Or there was the time Elijah put his head between his knees while praying for rain. (See 1 Kings 18:41–45.) People who saw that would have been insulted because that was the posture that women took on birthing stools in the Old Testament.

A lot of acts are messages in and of themselves. Why do we hold hands when we pray? Or kneel? It's an act of abasement, of humility, and it's a sign. Every kingdom is known by things like that. Those are salutations to enter. In certain regions in Africa that is how they greet one another, either by bowing or nodding or offering some other form of acknowledgment. Every culture has acts, so it makes sense that prophets, who are cultural agents of heaven, would sometimes move in acts to declare the word of the Lord.

Sometimes the need, the situation, and the moment will determine what prophetic expression God wants to employ. To be a seasoned prophet, you shouldn't be afraid to explore the different venues of the word of the Lord. This is important because some expressions won't work for certain audiences. Kings require counsel. They may not always respond to a declaration. Celebrities often require counsel, too, as do other high-profilers. It depends on the audience and what there is to do.

THE POWER OF
THE VOICE

Ultimately prophets are the mouthpiece and medium of the almighty God. Their voices carry power and should therefore be used accordingly—but also responsibly.

For example, I don't think people realize how many times we're told to shout up to God in the Book of Psalms. Shouting as a vocal response is scientific. It penetrates sound barriers and frequencies. "Shout unto God with the voice of triumph," Psalm 47:1 tells us. But think about the logic of that. Why do you need to tell the Lord you won? He already knows, so why do you need to shout it to Him?

Here's why. Shouting is an announcement to everything in the spirit world. Go through the Scriptures and see how many things we are told to do physically that we can theoretically do in our hearts. We could tell the Lord about His goodness in our hearts, yet we are told continually to tell Him out loud. The point is that the prophetic is really big. It's as big as God, which is why one can die still learning it. That technology and its range is beyond anything the earth can see. Until we're prophesying and thunder responds, we're not there.

That is why people were scared of Samuel. That brother got up and said, "Have I stolen your goats? Have I corrupted your village? No—on the contrary. Everything I've done has been to uphold the Lord's righteousness, and this day you rejected the Lord for being King over you." (See 1 Samuel 12.) Then Samuel told them, "'I will call to the LORD, that He may send thunder and rain. Then you will know and see that your wickedness is great which you have done in the sight of the LORD by asking for yourselves a king.' So Samuel called to the LORD, and the LORD sent thunder and rain that day; and all the people greatly feared the LORD and Samuel" (1 Sam. 12:17–18, NASB).

Prophetic expressions are to prove His word, because God confirms nothing more than He does His word.

Imagine that. The Bible talked about signs in the heavens and signs in the earth below. We need a species of prophet who will prophesy with signs following as the endorsement or the insignia of the Creator. "This prophecy will happen, and this will be a sign unto you." We need more of that!

We have so many examples of geophysical things that can occur through prophecy. Moses stretched out his staff over the water, and the Red Sea parted (Exod. 14). Elisha struck the water with Elijah's mantle, and the water parted, allowing Elisha to walk across (2 Kings 2:11–14). Do you realize what was happening? A body of water split as a result of the prophet's mantle.

All of what we've discussed here in this chapter are prophetic expressions that are the strict prophetic resources of prophets. These are supernatural providences of the prophets. God deposited abilities for those who are consecrated to prove His word. All of those prophetic expressions are to prove His word, because God confirms nothing more than He does His word.

CHAPTER 8

Words for the Wicked

I N ALL OF the prophetic studies and reading I've
done, I have only read about what God has to say
to wicked people one time. It is rarely talked about
directly or written about. But the predominant attitude in most prophetic streams is that God has only
one thing to say to the wicked, and that is, "Repent!"
This understanding of what God has to say to wicked
people leads people to utilize their ministerial time
by telling people what they need to know instead of
what God is saying—and a lot of times, what we think
people need to know is not what God is saying.

When you are a prophetic person, it is easy to conjure up prophetic things you discern about a person
and make them the word of the Lord. But just because
you can see or sense something about a person does
not mean it is the word of the Lord for them. Even
things that are revealed to you about a person may not

be the word of the Lord. When ministering to "wicked people," then, it is important to discern what is from God and what is from your flesh.

The goal of all revelation is relationship.

But let's back up for a second so I can help you understand what I mean by "word of the Lord." The word of the Lord is what God wants you to say or announce to a person. The key phrase here, though, is "what God wants you to say." As I said, you may have something revealed to you about a person for the sake of your knowing it, but you always have to challenge that revelation to ensure it is from God. A lack of caution, discretion, and discernment on the part of most prophetic ministers is why so many "wicked people" choose to stay wicked. They feel as if God has nothing more to say to them than "Repent or go to hell!" This is why we don't see as much redemption as we should.

THE GOAL IS
RELATIONSHIP

You must remember that the goal of all revelation is relationship. Let me say that again: *The goal of all revelation is relationship.*

So, if what is announced and prophesied over a person does not provide the opportunity for their repentance and redemption, which is always God's vision, then that "prophetic word" was not effective. A true prophetic word never assesses a person through their wickedness. It assesses them through the word of the Lord.

See, it is dangerous for us to create our own definitions of wickedness, because what we think is wicked and unjust may not be wicked and unjust in the eyes of God. When we create our own definitions of wickedness, we do so within the context of our feelings, our emotions, and our biases. We infuse our own insecurities, failures, and fears into it. It is imperative that we measure our definition of wickedness against the Word of God. If our definition of what we see as wicked is not in line with what God sees as wicked, we run the risk of illegitimately speaking on behalf of God.

Think about this example. Samuel, a man whose words the Lord never let fall to the ground (1 Sam. 3:19), was on the verge of anointing the wrong king because of how the person looked. Remember this? He was about to anoint one of David's older brothers! He got in front of the group of them and said about the first one, "Surely, this is the Lord's anointed." (See 1 Samuel 16:6.)

Did you catch that? The guy who never missed it prophetically was sure, but he was wrong! And the Lord responded to Samuel with a rebuke and said, "No, he's not. Do not look on his outer appearance or on his stature, for I have rejected him." (See 1 Samuel 16:7.) Then Samuel went to David and anointed him.

But here's a thought. What if God hadn't corrected Samuel? We would have had the wrong king!

So many of you are walking around with a "Surely, this is the Lord's anointed" mentality because of your lack of understanding. You allow what you see to dictate what you say. This example of Samuel with David proves God is not looking at people the way humans look at humans. Also, God is not distracted by people in the way humans can be distracted by them. People within the prophetic ministry need to more fully pick up the mind of Christ—to see people, their situations, and their futures through the lens of Christ.

GOD HAS A WORD

Now, right is still right and wrong is still wrong. Sin is sin, and holiness is holiness. But it is important to remember that God is not mute to the wicked. It is our biblical heritage that God has something to say to wicked men.

The Scriptures say in the Book of Isaiah, "Thine ears shall hear a word behind thee, saying, This is the way, walk ye in it" (30:21). So if God knows the way every man takes, then He has to provide a way for His word to work in the way every man takes and every decision a man makes. That's the power of the word.

Remember, too, when David said, "Where can I

flee from Your presence? If I ascend into heaven, You are there; *if I make my bed in hell…*" (Ps. 139:7–8, NKJV, emphasis added). If God does not have a word for the wicked, then why did David feel as if he could access God's presence and word there? What do you think David was talking about? Something must have happened that caused him to feel as if he *had* made his bed in hell (perhaps what happened with Bathsheba?), and something or someone must have pulled him out of that hell. What pulled him out? Nathan—the prophet who gave him a word. (See 2 Samuel 12:1–15.)

See? The wicked need a word too! You are not the only person that God wants to speak to. Nor are you the only person that God wants to nourish with His words. We have to stop being stingy and self-centered when it comes to the prophetic.

If our definition of what we see as wicked is not in line with what God sees as wicked, we run the risk of illegitimately speaking on behalf of God.

Think about it this way. If a wicked person is legitimately wicked, then where do they get the will to turn from their wickedness if not by the word of the Lord? So, not prophesying to wicked people robs us of powerful opportunities to win the war over a soul. "He who wins souls is wise," Proverbs tells us (11:30, NKJV). That means the wisdom of God wins souls. And that cannot be just tactical wisdom. It has to be eternal wisdom, the spirit of wisdom, even the word of wisdom, to win a soul.

Here's what you have to understand. If a soul must be won, that means there has to be a competition for it. And if there is a competition, there has to be a competitor—and there is a competition for every soul. There is a battle raging between the past and the present, evil and light, over every soul, a battle to take the soul out of darkness and into the marvelous light. The two power structures are in combat over every life.

What makes the difference? The word of the Lord!

You see, some people's hearts will never turn until they know God's opinion of them. Most people have lived their whole lives in response to or affected by, even groomed by, the opinions of people, and they have never been made aware of heaven's pure opinion of them. But remember what the Scriptures say: "I know the thoughts that I think toward you...thoughts of peace and not of evil" (Jer. 29:11, NKJV). And if you are never made aware that heaven has pure, objective opinions of you, then when you are faced with opportunities to turn, you probably will not turn.

YOU DON'T HAVE TO WORRY

Within the sin nature is its own condemnation system, called a conscience, so people live condemned whether or not we help them be condemned. Once a person has walked away from God or is living monstrously, there is always something in that soul reminding the person he has vacillated from truth.

In other words, the wicked don't need help feeling unworthy. That conscience in them already makes them feel disqualified. The constant questioning, the vacillation, the back-and-forth—that is what keeps them feeling as if they are not living up to the standard they should.

But this is why the wicked need a word too! Whether someone is perceived as wicked or not, the Bible judges the world. In John 17 when Jesus was praying, He said, "I'm not praying for the world. I'm praying so that you would keep them and preserve them from the evil one." (See John 17:9, 15.)

The conscience of the human race is a powerful thing because it will let you know when you have left God. Whether you know it or not, it will let you know. That's why people have to excessively smoke, drink, and have sex. It is all in an effort to suppress the conscience, which is full of the reminders of how the human self is decaying.

Think of it this way. There are people who don't have the Holy Spirit who will tell you, "My conscience wouldn't let me sleep," or, "My conscience wouldn't let me do it." What is that? It is the soul's way of reminding them of their call to righteousness.

So if all of this is true, why do the wicked need to

constantly be told about their wickedness? Now, there are obviously moments where a rebuke, a warning, or a judgment is necessary and needs to be said to a wicked person. If the person's actions are causing harm to others, often there will be a need to speak out. But rebuke and warning cannot be the only options we have when ministering to the wicked. Remember, the Word says God is "not willing that any should perish, but that all should come to repentance" (2 Pet. 3:9).

GOD'S HEART
FOR THE BACKSLIDDEN

I love how consistent God was throughout the Bible concerning the backslidden. Remember He called Israel not only a backslider (Hos. 4:16) but also His firstborn (Exod. 4:22–23). God made it abundantly clear that for every wicked person, for every person in sin, for every backslider, there is hope and a future.

And every wicked person deserves to hear about that hope and future! What did God do for the backslider? He sent covenant messengers, the prophets, to pull them back in. God's mindset concerning it all was, "You're going to backslide. I know that because I'm all-knowing. But I'm going to pull you back in through the word that is in My messengers." This is why the prophetic is so imperative when dealing with the wicked.

After all, if the prophetic cannot uphold the mystery

of redemption, the mystery of mercy, the mystery of the covenant heart of God, what is it worth? If we're not using our supernatural access to the future to return people to the heart of God, then aren't we just predicting events?

> *God made it abundantly clear that for every wicked person, for every person in sin, for every backslider, there is hope and a future.*

Here is the key to this whole thing. When we prophesy, what we do is let people know that coming out of wickedness is worth it! We let them know there is a world, an opportunity, and a wealth of circumstances available for every life that chooses to depart from wickedness.

WE MUST COMMIT TO THIS

The wicked really do need a word. But what does that mean for us, the church? It means we must commit ourselves to ministering prophetically to the wicked. We must dedicate ourselves to providing hope and a way of escape for those whose lives are controlled by wickedness.

It is bizarre that today's prophets in today's church have not been trained to use one of God's greatest tools to handle the wicked. We practice the prophetic on people who are saved and decided, but in order to occupy the full spectrum of the prophet's ministry, you must find yourself constantly showing the wicked the compassion and mercy of God through prophetic ministry.

The prophetic is a ministry of love. It was born in and meant to be executed through love. The prophetic ministry is supposed to give the wicked a glimpse of how much the Lord loves them. That's where it all began.

Whether or not the wicked need a word shouldn't even be a question. Everyone needs a word, wicked or not! But in order to understand that, you need a clear understanding of the mercy and compassion of God. Compassion deepens our prophetic ministry. The more compassionate and merciful we become, the more powerful our prophecies and judgments are. That's one of the secrets to my own efficacy in the prophetic, for the Lord has schooled me in mercy and compassion. One reason you may not be as effective with the wicked as you can or should be might be a lack of mercy and compassion.

The prophetic ministry is supposed to give the wicked a glimpse of how much the Lord loves them.

My advice to you would be to start there. Start with seeking a new level of mercy and compassion, not just for the wicked but for everyone you encounter. God has multiple, deep, rich, provoking words concerning everyone, and those words are filled with the love, mercy, and compassion of the Lord. If you do not have that in you, then your execution of those messages will not be effective.

What the wicked need more than anything is a word. They need hope. They need something to believe in. They need someone to assure them there is something better than what they are currently experiencing, and that it is available to them.

Will you dedicate yourself to this—to growing in mercy, growing in compassion, and ensuring that everyone you encounter, wicked or not, experiences the mercy of God?

Yes, the wicked need a word too! They don't need to be neglected, nor do they need to be ridiculed. They don't need your disgusted looks or your constant reminders that they are wicked and will end up in hell. What they need to hear is how God feels about them. What they need is for someone to paint a picture of how God sees them. What they need is someone whose ear is to God's heart.

My prayer is that we are able to come out of ourselves enough to hear what God truly has to say to the wicked. Just imagine how many people would choose Christ, choose salvation, and choose the will of God if they heard how He actually feels about them.

The problem is not the wicked. It's our lack of

commitment to providing the wicked with God's heart. The problem is not what God has to say or how much He has to say. He has never stopped talking. The problem is the lack of willing messengers, because if the wicked had a word, they wouldn't be wicked for long!

CHAPTER 9

A Decided Heart

W HEN IT COMES to hearing the voice of God well, is it God's volume or our sensitivity that changes? To be honest, I don't know that the Lord ever needs to adjust His volume. I think we need to change our sensitivity, which determines how well we hear.

Now, I believe in the audible voice of God, but I also believe the majority of people learn to know the voice of the Lord by devotion and, subsequently, by decision. They must choose to follow Him whole-heartedly. People who are undecided can't discern the voice of the Lord clearly because confusion in the heart can affect the clarity of the frequency by which we hear God. Sometimes when people's lives or hearts are unresolved, they hear God through whatever they are facing at the moment. Indecision makes it a challenge to perceive and know what God is saying.

That's why I believe decidedness is a key to prophetic clarity.

Decidedness is so important to God. To Him, a decided heart determines what a life can handle. Once a heart is decided, heaven watches to see what more that heart is ready to know.

A lot of people get really frustrated because they don't know what's next, but the key to receiving details from God is to make a decision for God. The more decided a heart is, the more God trusts that heart to handle details. That is powerful to consider. In some lives and some instances, if there is confusion, there may also be indecision. Again, decision is the key to clarity from the Lord.

There are people familiar with prophetic things who still have not achieved the degree of clarity that they could. That is because clarity is not just an issue of the mind. It is also an issue of the heart. The heart is where clarity is born. The heart ends up affecting the mind, but it also turns so many directions for so many different things.

The key to receiving details from God is to make a decision for God.

In this final chapter we're going to see what helps you develop a decided heart for God. It will make all the difference in your prophetic ministry.

NAMING GOD

The Lord really wants His faithfulness to settle the heart. The way we settle our hearts is through reflection on the actions of God. "Praise ye the LORD," Psalm 150 says. "Praise him for his mighty acts: praise him according to his excellent greatness" (vv. 1–2).

We are told to talk of the acts of God from generation to generation, and we are told to do this in order to settle the heart. This is not meant to just give successive generations a story line. It is not just testimony we are meant to pass down. What we pass down through our testifying of God's mighty acts is decidedness. Mothers and fathers and families have the power, through their conversations with their children, to release decidedness.

A lot of kids who grow up in church are familiar with what they believe from a Christian point of view, but they have not really seen or received decidedness. Telling of the acts of God from one generation to the next is one way God brings a heart into decidedness.

That is so powerful, because decidedness is the door to revelation. What you decide determines what will speak to you. To choose anything other than God will give that thing volume.

PRAISE AND WORSHIP

If you reduce it to the lowest common denominator, daily devotion is daily decidedness. To pray, to worship, and to seek the Lord in the Scriptures is the reinforcement of decidedness. There are people who have made decisions, but they don't decide daily. It is a choice.

Have you studied the devotional habits in the psalms? The psalmists wrote about habits all the time. They were powerful ministers of devotion and decidedness. Study the psalms and notice how the psalmists wrote about worship, lyricism, praise, and adoration throughout each one.

If you reduce it to the lowest common denominator, daily devotion is daily decidedness. To pray, to worship, and to seek the Lord in the Scriptures is the reinforcement of decidedness.

The point is not just getting human beings to adore God but to "decide" Him—to choose Him daily by seeking Him in prayer, praise, and worship. People adore God *after* they decide Him. If we teach the psalms and psalmistry and the ministry of the psalmist like it's the resource to make God feel better about Himself, then we don't really see what praise and worship do to the human condition. Praise and worship are powerful in heaven, but they are more transforming to the human heart than to God.

The Bible talks about how God resides or dwells

in the praises of His people. (See Psalm 22:3.) This has to do with proximity, nearness, closeness. Praise and worship are transformational to a life. A life that is surrendered through praise and worship will be changed over time. Praise and worship bring us closer and closer to God.

Praise and worship help a person keep God in the right purview. Worship is about abasing yourself, saying, "He is God; I am not. He is on the throne; I am on the altar." That's the salience of worship. It hammers down the untransformed areas in a life. This is important in correlating praise and worship to prophetic sensitivity. The Bible talks about making Jerusalem a praise in the earth (Isa. 62:7). As a person is surrendered through daily and consistent worship practices, her life starts to change. The proximity barriers separating that person from God change.

I really believe that a part of the next move of God in the earth is revolutionizing what people believe about devotion and devotedness. There are so many scriptures about doing things with your whole heart; about loving the Lord your God with all your heart, soul, and strength. I don't believe we humans (including Christians) have seen many people master wholeheartedness. We haven't seen what it means to love the Lord with all one's heart, soul, strength, and might and what that requires. That is not an easy feat. It really does require everything out of the human nature to learn to love, respond to, and interact with God the way our hearts need to.

STAY CLOSE

The more distant a person's heart is from God, the greater the likelihood that person lacks detail or clarity in his or her communication with God. It is not as easy to hear someone from a distance, and the same is true of God. He does not speak as clearly when we are at a distance. He will say certain things: "Repent." "Turn." "Come." "Choose." But the closer a heart gets to God, the more specific He gets, and the more we will discern His voice. And the way to draw your heart close to God is through praise and worship. They are so important.

Many people don't hear God as clearly as they could because their hearts are distant from Him. Revelation 4:1 says, "Come up here, and I will show you" (AMP). Proximity determines volume. How close you are to the Lord matters. People who are not as close to God as they should be or could be often make decisions in confusion or doubt. We even see this in people throughout the Scriptures. The closer you get to God, the clearer His voice becomes.

The more distant a person's heart is from God, the greater the likelihood that person lacks clarity in his or her communication with God. It is not as easy to hear someone from a distance.

If you think about it, even in the natural sense, your closeness to a person teaches you to know that individual's tone and voice and how he or she says things. When you're dealing with language, you're not just dealing with dialogue. You're also dealing with dialect. This is why three or four different categories of Hispanic nationals—for example, Mexicans, Puerto Ricans, Dominicans, and Cubans—all speak the same language but have a dialect native to where they are from. This means different words can be used interchangeably for each of them. For example, Mexicans elongate things. Puerto Ricans chop things up. They do it real fast. Same language. Same origin. Different approaches to that language. The same is true in heaven. Heaven has not only dialogue but also dialect.

GOD'S TONE

God not only speaks in His voice; He also has a tone. He says different things in different ways. That is a powerful part of prophetic clarity. A major reason prophets are necessary is to interpret the mood of heaven. See, people who are distant from God don't realize heaven has emotions and moods! But if you think about it, there are moments in the Scriptures when God said, "And it grieved him" or "And it repented the LORD that he had made man on the earth" (Gen. 6:6). God has feelings. You start to know them and decipher them, just as a person does with a spouse—where you learn what they mean not just when they speak but also by their body language. Children also do this with their parents; they learn what it means when Mom or Dad calls for them one way versus another. Some people know that if Mom uses their middle name, they're in trouble, no matter how old they get!

I think that sometimes we read the Scriptures without considering the tone God is using, which is why we miss a lot of revelation. We appreciate the text but not the tone. For example, when God said about Jesus, "This is my beloved Son, in whom I am well pleased" (Matt. 3:17), I doubt very seriously that He said it the way many of us say it. How many of us even read it?

See, we read Scripture through the lens of our culture and experience, so it flavors how we approach it. You have to really step out of the American or contemporary culture to engage the text of Scripture as it was written.

Let's think about this. If we consider everything God went through and set up to bring the Messiah to earth—the generation that got to push the Messiah out of the invisible world into the visible world; how it took getting Him all the way through forty-two generations, with everything that was prophesied and that He did—would God make an announcement by simply saying, "This is my Son; I am well pleased"? I believe it was one of the loudest things God ever said!

Normally when we read about the audible voice of God, the Lord is speaking to a person. A cynic evaluating those instances may or may not be willing to acknowledge that those moments happened. But if several people stood watching the same event and all of them recorded that God said something, what He said had to be so earth-shattering—like, geophysically shattering—that it made them remember what He meant. I think that was the case here. This was probably one of the most powerful statements God ever made, so much so that it couldn't have been said in somebody's heart. It had to have been audible.

God not only speaks in His voice; He also has a tone. He says different things in different ways. A major reason prophets are necessary is to interpret the mood of heaven.

If you think about it, God's statement over Jesus was not for Jesus, or else He would've said it only to Jesus. That very same sentence could have been said to Jesus' heart in the wilderness or prior to His going to the wilderness, when He was studying and debating with the Jewish scholars before He went to the water. If the statement were made for His personal affirmation, God didn't need to speak so publicly.

But those words were spoken to set the stage for the story that was about to unfold. God was setting up the production for what they were about to see happen through the life of the Messiah. In saying, "This is my beloved Son, in whom I am well pleased," God was setting the precedent that He was pleased with what would take place through the life of Jesus.

All of this is to say that God's voice has a tone, and God's voice has volume. There are times when He says things in different ways. The question is, Are we sensitive enough to hear Him?

DO NOT FALTER

For this last part I want to take us to 1 Kings 19, which is the story of Elijah meeting God in the cave. But to understand why this story is important, we first need to lean in to Elijah's sermon on Mount Carmel.

God's voice has a tone, and God's voice has volume. He says things in different ways. The question is, Are we sensitive enough to hear Him?

In 1 Kings 18, if you remember, Elijah called "the four hundred and fifty prophets of Baal, and the four hundred prophets of Asherah, who eat at Jezebel's table" to meet him on Mount Carmel. So he was dealing with a whole prophetic institution of several of the deities. But Elijah never even addressed the prophets. He never said, "You wicked prophets of Ashtoreth." What did he say? "How long will you halt?" (See 1 Kings 18:21.)

It's amazing that with all of those dramatics—you've

got altars and bulls and folks cutting themselves and bleeding—his message was about decisions. If I were putting myself in that scene, I would've preached about anything. God was about to answer by fire, so Elijah could have come up with a lot of things to preach. He could have preached, "You are in a drought, but you're coming out." They were literally in a whole drought, and the heavens weren't going to open until after this. But Elijah's statement was, "How long are you going to halt between two opinions? If God be God, follow Him."

You see, this issue of decisions, decision-making, and decidedness really does affect clarity when it comes to hearing God's voice. Think about it. If you have resolved to not want Him, why would He give you clarity? It makes no sense. That's the whole story in the Book of Ezekiel. God said to Ezekiel, "Son of man, when the children of the house of Israel come before you to inquire of Me, answer them according to the idols that are in their hearts." (See Ezekiel 14:1–5.) What is that about? It has to be the absence of clarity.

This is a powerful thing to study. It's not just about quieting the heart or quieting the environment or lighting a candle. It really is about bringing the heart as close as possible to the Lord, and doing it every day.

Now, this is why praise and worship are so powerful, because they do that. Worship is the instrument that brings the heart closer to God. As you learn praise and as you learn worship, you learn a daily discipline of moving your heart closer to Him. And the closer that heart gets, the more confident you get.

When it comes to the prophetic, the mechanics of prophetic ministry are not necessarily going to help you develop sensitivity. Oh, they can activate you in a way, but a heart that is distant from God will never know the same clarity that a surrendered heart will. Never. Because it's difficult to try to persuade a person about a God that you are still distant from. You can't convince any crowd or any listener of somebody who has not really won you.

We need a revelation of New Testament persuasion. How many times did Paul reiterate how persuaded he was? He lived a convinced life, a decided life. Nobody really uses the apostle Paul as an example of prophetic clarity, but to be honest, we really should. This guy summarizes the whole of the Old Testament with a gospel of grace. If that's not clarity, I don't know what is. I mean, this brother spends some years in some desert and comes out with a revelation because he didn't have the same challenges or history as the Twelve. He came out with fresh clarity because God had less to convince him of.

People ask me all the time, "What's the secret to clearly discerning the voice of the Lord?" I could talk about having certain lights and a particular type of music and all that, but let me tell you, the real secret to prophetic clarity is the environment of your life.

It really is about bringing the heart as close as possible to the Lord, and doing it every day. This is why praise and worship are so powerful, because they do that.

What is in the way of God being able to say what He really wants to say? What does He have to question? Think about the generations of people in your own family whose hearts have been distant from God. You can see it by the decisions that they made—the things they did, the stuff they entertained, the stuff they welcomed into their lives, the stuff they chose to want more of. A distant heart won't have prophetic clarity.

Now, when people hear stuff like that, the instant human reaction is to strain, to muster up energy and hurry up and work toward getting closer. But when you make heart decisions, it almost becomes its own source of energy. A decided heart will wake up early in the morning, because it is training your body to want certain things. The body acts out the decisions of the heart. "As [a man] thinketh in his heart, so is he" (Prov. 23:7). The physical body is always going to manifest the meditation of the heart.

All of that affects prophetic value. What did Elijah say? "How long will you halt between two opinions?

If God be God, follow Him." He corrected a whole nation that was vacillating between God and gods. And after he preached it, the fire fell, which shows that the key to the fire of God is a decided people. People who are not decided will never know His fire. It would consume them wholly. You have to know the power of decision, being persuaded, and being resolved.

REMOVE THE MOUNTAINS

What happened next? We go to 1 Kings 19, where Elijah met God in a cave. The text says, "And he came thither unto a cave, and lodged there; and, behold, the word of the LORD came to him, and he said unto him, What doest thou here, Elijah?" (v. 9).

"What are you doing here, Elijah?" This opens up the power of self-awareness—being able to know where you are. God asks Elijah, "Why are you here? At what place are you lodging?" Again, God wanted Elijah to assess his environment. Why are you where you are? If you want to trace this issue of prophetic sensitivity in your life, you need to find out where you feel at home—your life lodging, in a way—and what makes you feel safe and secure.

Many people have trouble hearing God because of their inability to see past themselves— where they are, what they've done, what they need, and even what is after them.

So God asked, "What are you doing here, Elijah?" And this is how Elijah responded: "I have been very jealous for the LORD God of hosts: for the children of Israel have forsaken thy covenant, thrown down thine altars, and slain thy prophets with the sword; and I, even I only, am left; and they seek my life, to take it away" (1 Kings 19:10).

"And he said, 'Go forth, and stand upon the mount before the LORD'" (v. 11). First of all, let me show you the nature of noise. Elijah just set up a very noisy scene for God to talk within. Look at all these statements he made. "I've been jealous for the LORD God of hosts." Personal credit. "Now I'm alone." Alienation. "They have killed everybody else like me. Nobody's made it before." Huh? "They murdered them with a sword." That's probably a manifestation of terror.

The most powerful word in that verse is *I*. *I* am left. *I* have been very jealous for the Lord God of hosts. *I* only am left. *I*.

That is one of the things that gets in the way of prophetic clarity, for sure. Many people have trouble hearing God because of their inability to see past themselves—where they are, what they've done, what they need, and even what is after them. Elijah said, "They're after me." A lot of people miss God for fear of what's coming for them.

Now, hear this. Whatever you fear is after you has a volume. It has a sound. It has a tone. If you are afraid of something, the thing that you fear is after you. This is why it is so important to be rid of fear: so you can discern the voice of the Lord. It is easy to listen more to what's after you than the direction you were given for where you're supposed to be going. If you have a constant reminder that something is after you that could kill you, ruin you, or harm you like it did everybody else, that will always seem louder than God's voice.

But now it gets interesting. Think about the context of the conversation. God said, "Elijah, why are you here?" And Elijah said, "Jezebel has killed all the prophets of God." That didn't answer the question, but it was the logic behind where he was, his life's environment. He was thinking, *It happened to them; it's going to happen to me.*

Now, I love what the Lord made him do. He said, "Go forth, and stand upon the mount before the LORD" (1 Kings 19:11). The reality is that sometimes you have to do things in order to see things. If you don't deliberately act, you won't see what God has for you. For example, Abraham didn't see the ram and the bush until he went out on top of the mountain. In Revelation 4, John didn't get the rest of the revelation until he went up higher. This conversation Elijah was having with God had to be taking place on a low level, because God told Elijah to come up to the mount in order to meet the level of clarity he was going to need for his next victory.

What this proves, by the way, is that God will talk to you when you are at your lowest—but that doesn't mean that's all He has to say. See, until you come out of what is your lowest-level anything, you are going to miss a certain degree of clarity.

Sometimes you have to do things in order to see things. If you don't deliberately act, you won't see what God has for you.

Think about how many people to whom God is saying, "Come up and present yourself on the mount before the Lord," but they aren't doing it because they're OK with the level of conversation they have where they are.

But what happens when a heart responds and obeys, and goes up and stands before the mount of the Lord? Think about the mechanics of this. God is God, right? He's God. He could've used anything. As a matter of fact, an angel had just been to visit Elijah to feed him and give him bread and coal and water. (See 1 Kings 19:5–8.) The angel could have given him the message. But God wanted Elijah to take responsibility for the next level of clarity he received. So God told him, "You have to go up. Present yourself before Me." Isn't that crazy, how the Lord wouldn't talk anymore until Elijah changed where he was?

So God said, "Come up. Present yourself before the Lord." And when Elijah got there, verse 11 says: "And, behold, the LORD passed by, and a great and strong wind rent the mountains, and brake in pieces the rocks before the LORD; but the LORD was not in the wind."

Listen to me. It is possible that God could be moving and you still don't hear Him. But God moved in order to deal with what was in the way of Elijah's ability to hear. Why was there a need to tear the mountains up? Why was there a need to break rocks?

First of all, can we just talk scientifically for a minute? Can you imagine how strong a wind had to be to break a mountain? That wasn't a breeze.

But here again, we have to notice something. Changing your level, like Elijah did, is enough to get God to move, but it still may not be enough to get Him to talk. Elijah moved, and God moved too—but still Elijah did not hear God's voice. It wasn't in the wind or in the earthquake or in the fire. Now, maybe you have moved your level to hear God, but you're just not hearing what you need to hear. Yet God is moving. Why is He moving? To deal with mountains and rocks.

Didn't Elijah just say he was scared? Could it be that the reason he was there to begin with was to find safety? How do we know he didn't find safety or protection in the mountains or the rocks? But when he went up to the top of the mount to present himself before the Lord, what happened? The wind came and tore the rock, but God wasn't in it.

What does that mean? Put yourself in the text. What would you have done if you were Elijah? That strong gust of wind tore rock into pieces. God was showing that He is the God of the rocks. He's God over mountains. It's like He was saying, "Anything that's in the way of you perceiving what I'm doing next, I have the power to move and break it so you can hear Me."

Do you know what God was doing, for real? He was regaining lost trust.

Because of the war that happened in 1 Kings 18, in his heart Elijah had lost a measure of confidence in God. That's what trauma does. That's what a traumatic season does. That's what seeing bloodshed does, even if you come out alive. He came out alive but battle-fatigued. His exhaustion from fighting affected his confidence in God. So God did in 1 Kings 19 a different version of what He did in 1 Kings 18. He showed His strength. And when He did, Elijah became confident in what God would say next.

Look at this. God was not in the rocks, and He was not in the wind, and then there was an earthquake. He started all kind of stuff. *Boom, boom, boom.* Was this another geophysical judgment? No, because there was nobody to be judged. What was God doing? He was showing that no matter the elements around you, He is more powerful than where you have lodged.

But after the wind and the earthquake and the fire, there was a still, small voice. Now, let me ask you a question. Are earthquakes loud? Absolutely. Wind? Yes, especially one with that degree of strength.

I believe the still, small voice was louder than the rocks. It had to be. Because whatever changed in Elijah's sensitivity changed after he was convinced God was God over where he was.

The text doesn't tell us what God said in that still, small voice, but we can imagine it because we see how Elijah responded to whatever the small voice said. Let's imagine it. After this fire, a still, small voice. Look at 1 Kings 19:13: "And it was so, when Elijah heard it, that he wrapped his face in his mantle, and went out, and stood in the entering in of the cave. And, behold, there came a voice unto him, and said, What doest thou here, Elijah?"

Now, the first time God asked him, "What are you doing here?" we saw no mention of the mantle. Do you understand what I'm telling you? The first time God dealt with Elijah, He was dealing with the man. But this second time, whatever God said to Elijah was enough for him to pick up his mantle. It's as if God had said to him, "You still have work to do."

We don't know what God actually said to Elijah, of course, but Elijah's reaction was, "Let me put this mantle on." Isn't that crazy? That's what the scripture says: "He wrapped his face in his mantle." Whatever that exchange between them was, it had to remind Elijah of the responsibility yet to come, because he clothed himself up.

Even so, God still asked him, "Where are you now?" But see, I think this time was different. When God speaks to you when you're not under that mantle or your assignment, it's different from when He speaks to you when you've said yes to it. There was a different degree of restored confidence in Elijah. I mean, if you're complaining about prophets dying, the last thing you're going to do in that moment of discouragement is put on a prophet's mantle. But whatever God said in that still, small voice was louder than the rocks, the earthquake, and the fire.

That's the nature of noise. God spoke in His way, and it impacted the heart. It overcame what Elijah could see. I don't know about you, but I would be scared to death in an earthquake. Or of a rock being divided into pieces. But whatever Elijah heard from God was more powerful than what he saw in the rocks and the fires.

There are probably millions of people around the world who are stuck in that prior verse, where God is asking them, "What are you doing here?" And they never make it past God's authority over the rocks, the fire, the wind, or whatever else is in their way. But if they would stay long enough to see the move take its full effect—to see the move of the Spirit, the move of

God—then they would reposition themselves and put on their mantles. That is a powerful thing.

It is important that you not lose clarity, because somebody else's victory is in it.

Here's the next thing God spoke to Elijah after that conversation. God told him, "Go find Elisha and anoint him prophet in your stead." (See 1 Kings 19:15–16.) Why? Because Elijah's assignment to Elisha was even more important than his war with Jezebel. Had Elijah lost his focus in that moment of lost clarity in between 1 Kings 18 and 19, he would not have been able to mentor Elisha, and Elisha may not have walked in a double portion of the anointing on Elijah's life.

See, Elisha was more important. That was Elijah's next assignment. That is why he had to rewrap himself in that mantle. He had to clothe himself and then bring somebody else into it. And here is what this means for you: Whatever you are going through right now is going to become the garment by which you robe somebody you don't even know yet. It is important that you not lose clarity, because somebody else's victory is in it.

CONCLUSION

God used prophets throughout the Scriptures to bring deliverance and direction, and He still wants to use prophets to proclaim His word and His will, and to reveal His plans and purposes. He has more to say than what we've been hearing. The future holds more than houses, cars, and spouses for the people of God. It holds moves of God unlike anything we've ever seen.

If you have felt muzzled or marginalized in your prophetic call, I pray this book has helped you find the courage to take your stand, find a mentor to help train you, and walk in the fullness of your assignment, because the world and the body of Christ need you. The church cannot reach its full potential without prophets. We need every member, every ministry gift, and every office to be in full operation to see all that God has planned to do in the earth come to fruition.

We need God's prophets to come out of hiding. We need them to walk in the fullness of their calling. We need them to hear from heaven and proclaim the word of the Lord. In short, we need them to accept their prophetic responsibility.

About the Author

MATTHEW L. STEVENSON III is a global influencer, culturalist, and visionary who has been violently raised up by God during this complex moment in history. As a decorated scholar and former professional academic, he uses his background to complement his leadership style and approach to strategy. He has traveled to nineteen nations and published seven books. His public ministry dates back to 1999, and he has served as the founder and senior pastor of All Nations Worship Assembly for fifteen years. He is gaining international momentum as the founder of one of the nation's largest and fastest-growing urban Charismatic movements—All Nations Worship Assembly, which is one church in ten locations and home to over fifteen thousand people.

Stevenson's ministry is marked by powerful preaching, a bold delivery, and unusual supernatural activity. Intensely gifted in the prophetic, he has dramatically impacted thousands around the world with his timely, direct, and specific prophetic words. Stevenson actively provides spiritual support to entertainers, professional athletes, politicians, and business executives. He is an apostolic leader with the Father's heart entrenched in his life. As an overseer, he is responsible for many churches through the All Nations Network, a conglomerate of autonomous ministries that look to Stevenson for spiritual covering. His greatest accomplishment and joy are serving his wife in life and love and being a rock and provider for his three natural children.